THIRSTING

for

LIFE

and

REALITY

KARL LOESCHER

CREATION
HOUSE

THIRSTING FOR LIFE AND REALITY by Karl Loescher
Published by Creation House
A Charisma Media Company
600 Rinehart Road
Lake Mary, Florida 32746
www.charismamedia.com

Unless otherwise noted, all Scripture quotations are from the King James Version of the Bible.

Scripture quotations marked NKJV are from the New King James Version of the Bible. Copyright © 1979, 1980, 1982 by Thomas Nelson, Inc., publishers. Used by permission.

Design Director: Bill Johnson
Cover design by Nathan Morgan

Library of Congress Cataloging-in-Publication Data: 2011932336
International Standard Book Number: 978-1-61638-621-4

First edition

11 12 13 14 15 — 987654321
Printed in Canada

DEDICATION

I dedicate this book to the woman whom God placed me under shortly after my conversion in 1995. After five years of being under her mentorship and guidance she passed on to be with the Lord. Her Spirit-filled life offered me great nourishment at a time when I needed to grow. She rebuked me, challenged me, inspired me, believed in me and gave me direction. Our conversations were always lively and drew us into discussing the depths of Christ. Her greatest desire was to see others move up in Christ and pass it on.

I also dedicate this book to my wife who has stood with me through the hard mistakes and trials that were endured. She has helped me type and edit the content of this book from my handwritten notes.

I further dedicate this book to all those who are hungry and thirsty and are looking for life and reality. For those who are waiting for change and a great shaking in the church. So be it, let it begin. Let all those who have an ear to hear, let them hear.

This is for You Lord!

ACKNOWLEDGEMENTS

I F IT WEREN'T for God's gifts I would know nothing and be as the ostrich (Job 39:17). Thank you Jesus for making me more than an ostrich; for opening my eyes and heart to Your plan. The end is near and You don't make mistakes with anyone's life. Nothing is by chance and Your timing is impeccable. You told that You would perfect men's hearts regarding this book.

As you have cast the seeds of all mankind into the soil of life; take this seed within these pages and cast it into the hearts of Your people. Cause it to germinate and grow into maturity, that the end may come. To You, Father, Son and Holy Spirit, Author of Life, be all the glory.

Amen.

Thank you Creation House and staff for all your help making this book a reality.

CONTENTS

FOREWORD

THIS IS A great book! I first met Karl Loescher through my itinerate prophetic ministry years ago, at which time God had imparted a word for ministry that would bless and inspire the Lord's people in the direction they should go. I believe that through this book, this word, among others spoken to Karl over the years is coming to pass.

Reading this work will inspire you and change how you see things! I'm not an avid reader; so going into this I doubted my wisdom in agreeing to review this book. Yet as I read and re-read it, I was happy I had taken on this project. This was a time of learning for me, and it was a time of enjoying the revelation God has given to my friend Karl.

Karl's calling and gifting empowers him to impart to people through writing. This book is well written presenting a strong case for the subject at hand. This is a thorough study, involving a tremendous amount of research balanced with much scripture and insight.

I believe these are things that people should know and I encourage the reader to press through to the end; you will be greatly blessed. I feel there is an added benefit from a re-read, to be able to get all the truth and revelation contained herein. Karl has brought us great truth, and has fully explored it. I want to personally thank him for the effort and time he took to get this accomplished.

I appreciate that this book can speak to new believers to create a good foundation of truth as well as those who have been Christians for many years that need a deeper walk with God. There is truly something for everyone. I believe God is raising Karl up to be a voice of change in this hour that will take on subjects that people have institutionalized or become complacent with.

Pray therefore, and ask the Lord to help you glean what He is saying to you in the words of this book, you will be presently surprised as I was. You and I need this revelation. With it we will grow in Christ and experience new realms of glory and anointing! Enjoy!

—Mike Boland
Over forty years in ministry
Planted two churches
Senior pastor thirteen years in Texas, Oklahoma, and Kansas
Elder and on staff with Dutch Sheets
Twenty-eight years traveling in prophetic Ministry

INTRODUCTION

IN SEPTEMBER 2007 I had a dream. My wife and I were standing in a lineup waiting for lunch in a gym. A concession window was along one of the walls and there was a side door that led into the kitchen, which was standing open to see into.

I knew that the lunches were being served in brown paper bags. The lineup was quite long. We were waiting and waiting for someone to start serving but nothing was happening. Suddenly, through the open door I saw a man dash back and forth quickly, and he was holding two brown paper bags. I thought that now perhaps the line would start moving. But to my disappointment he just ran out a side door that led outside and was gone.

I wondered what was going on. So I went in the open door and looked around. It was a little room with a counter. To my amazement there was a table and chairs right in front of the concession window with three men sitting around it. These men were the kitchen staff and they were sitting there playing cards instead of serving. They were completely ignoring the lineup of people in front of the window who were waiting for their lunch!

I rebuked them and said, "Wouldn't it be better to be closed than to let the people think you are open and then feed them nothing?" Then I awoke.

As you begin to read this book there may be things that will cause the spiritual ears to tingle. I believe at the very least what is written will challenge the reader to reach their God-given promises and move towards maturity if read with an open heart. There may be things that are downright frightful to some and this I believe is because the church has been existing on the elementary things of Christ, which are necessary for the basics of a Christian walk; but there needs to be more meat given in due season. Nevertheless because of this there have been various aspects of the life of Christ that have become predominant over the others, unwittingly separating His life into the things that are palatable and easy to digest.

There are many facets to the life of Christ both in His earthly life as well as His heavenly one. We must draw out all the aspects that surround Christ's life before we can see God's purpose for His life as a whole; because it is to bring us into the life we were meant to walk in. Each of these things is of equal importance for the preparation of His people in receiving God's fullness.

There are things that Jesus fulfilled in His earthly life that I believe are overlooked and not recognized for one reason or another. Therefore, we have not seen what God's plan is in totality for it to be applied practically to our lives. I present to you a more in-depth prophetic revelation into God's purpose through Christ's accomplishment for us, drawn from the Scriptures, as well as what I have received in my heart. Therefore, I endeavor to put into perspective what God truly gave us through the Son.

Therefore, the purpose of this book is clear: to give the church vision and direction, that the spiritually hungry may be nourished.

I believe that believers in Jesus Christ cannot truly understand their destiny found in God's heart, if the ultimate purpose for man is misunderstood. God does not see as we see. He not only sees the past, present and future, He sees epochs in history, though thousands of years exist between them. God sees the correlation between one and another. If we misunderstand what God sees and what His intentions have been for man, we are in danger of delusion and missing the epoch that will seal the end of the age.

There is also the danger of delusion on an individual level as well as the body as a whole, especially when walls are built up by the precepts of men and we teach and prophesy from this position. We speak and "hear" from that which is dear to our hearts, but not necessarily the truth as in the case of Ahab in 1 Kings 22:4–28. Also:

Where there is no vision, the people perish.

—PROVERBS 29:18

If God's purpose is not understood it is like having a map without a compass to point in a definite direction in which to seek. Therefore, in the truest sense of the pastoral spirit, I humbly present this book to you.

Feed my sheep.
—JOHN 21:16 (SEE JOHN 21:15–17, JEREMIAH 3:15)

Chapter 1

DISAPPOINTED

It was a calm summer evening when I pulled into the parking lot across from the church. This particular church was holding revival services for a few weeks and I was invited to come. Since I did not have a church background and had only recently been converted to Christ, I was taking in the services with great excitement and joy. This night though, I was filled with expectation for what was about to take place. The previous evening the announcement went forth that they would be praying for people to receive the baptism in the Holy Spirit. I waited patiently throughout the service for this pinnacle moment when people would come forward to have prayer for this. The time finally came and I made my way up to the front. As I stood in line waiting my turn I was filled with anticipation. Then one of the workers came to me and told me to open my mouth and let a sound come out. I did this till I formed something I never heard before, consisting of a weird sentence or two. "There, that was it," I was assured; the work was apparently done and I was sent back to my seat, *heavyhearted*.

Did I know enough about the baptism in the Holy Spirit and what it meant? A person comes for prayer, opens their mouth, speaks something foreign (that is immediately taken for "tongues") and there, you are now considered *baptized in the Holy Spirit*? Was that it? Was that all? Is that all there is for the Christian life? This was totally disappointing! As the evening drew to a close and people spilled out into the parking lot I drove home taking my disappointment with me.

I actually thought that the living God, Creator of the universe, Creator of you and me, all-powerful, all-knowing, in all His fullness was going to come and live in little old me; that it is no longer I who live, but Christ who lives in me! Therefore I was left with a choice, believe the status quo or what was real to my heart. I have never been a person who has accepted the "norm" just because someone said I should or because the masses were raving over it; even before I knew Christ. No, I could not go against what my heart was becoming full of, what was being birthed within me whether I understood it or not and no one was going to convince me otherwise.

NOTHING MORE

A person can only give what he himself has received; nothing more. If I have received a cup of water, I can then give you a cup of water to quench your thirst. If I have a pitcher, I can give it to you till you are satisfied. But if I have a wellspring, I can satisfy the thirst of all who come, myself included. When Jesus called His disciples to Himself and gave them an "entry-level" power and authority over unclean spirits and sickness, they gave that out until they reached the limit of that which was given to them. Jesus drew a line and knew that at some point they would need to call upon Him for more. He expected them to perform the task given to them to do, but they came to the place where they could no longer.

The purpose wasn't that they would always be dependent upon Jesus to come to their rescue, but rather that they could be made aware of their own lack! I believe that because of the slowness of our hearts to understand God, He will give us an "entry-level" gift to use. This continues until we hit closed doors and nothing from the past seems to work for us now and we too reach our limit. Therefore, this wakes us up to needing *something more*. Unfortunately, institutions and doctrines are built around the "entry level," causing the entry level to lose its purpose as a "wake-up call" entirely. At that point people either lose hope or are entrenched in formality and tradition and say we have reached the end.

I too, when I came forward to receive the baptism of the Holy Spirit, was like the father in the Bible who had the son with a dumb spirit and came to the disciples of Jesus to heal him. Remember, the disciples could not do what the father requested for his son. They were at *their limit*. At that time in my life I did as the father had done and turned to Jesus for an answer.

Chapter 2

WHEN LANGUAGE LOSES ITS ESSENTIAL MEANING

Go to, let us go down, and there confound their language, that they may not understand one another's speech.

—Genesis 11:7

Have you ever had someone who spoke another language try to explain something to you? You hear their voice and the sounds that come out of their mouth attach meaning to objects around them according to their own understanding, but you do not know what they are.

> Therefore if I know not the meaning of the voice, I shall be unto him that speaketh a barbarian, and he that speaketh shall be a barbarian unto me.
>
> —1 Corinthians 14:11

If you teach someone from a foreign land who is newly learning your language, that an apple is round, orange and fuzzy, when they go to the store looking for an apple they will come back with what you described. But this would most certainly not be an apple. Suppose you taught 10,000 foreigners the same thing. Guess what? Peaches have become apples for that group of people. When these people go and buy an "apple" they are still coming home with something, but not an authentic apple.

Suppose I was an Israelite and you were a stranger who came to me from a strange land and you received God as Ruth in the Bible did. You agreed to learn the Law of Moses, and I taught you that it was acceptable to eat *leavened* bread during the feast of unleavened bread. I would most certainly be the cause of your death. (See Exodus 12:15.)

7

These two illustrations are using blatant lies, but the consequences are equally troubling when only half the truth is provided and you are led to believe otherwise. Let's look at a couple of these illustrations from the Bible.

> And David said unto Ahimelech the priest, The king hath commanded me a business, and hath said unto me, Let no man know anything of the business where about I send thee....give me five loaves of bread in mine hand.
>
> —1 Samuel 21:2–3

David was on an urgent matter indeed. He was fleeing for his life, but he was not commanded by the king although he said he was. Ahimelech **believed** David and upon Saul inquiring of the matter, commanded the death of not only Ahimelech but of all the priests of Nob. David responded to the son of Ahimelech who had escaped:

> I have occasioned the death of all the persons [priests] of thy father's house.
>
> —1 Samuel 22:22, emphasis added

Again, the serpent said to Eve:

> Hath God said, Ye shall not eat of every tree of the garden?
>
> —Genesis 3:1

Eve responded that she would die if she ate the fruit of the Tree of Knowledge of Good and Evil, to which the serpent answered:

> Ye shall not surely die. For God doth know that in the day ye eat thereof, then your eyes shall be opened, and ye shall be as gods, knowing good and evil.
>
> —Genesis 3:4–5

This does have some truth to it, but not the whole truth. We know that the devil deceives many by providing only half the truth. The true meaning of the thing becomes twisted and the outcome becomes unexpected. Therefore, half-truths can become what is believed to be the truth; and have devastating results.

Now let's imagine for a minute that the tree of life in the middle of the garden only bore fruit once a year for one hour. It's possible they would have been caught up with the duties of the garden, and it could've been less desirable to wait for a fruit to grow on a tree that seemed "barren" a majority of the year. If they had realized what the eating of the tree of life meant, which we will discuss later, they would have left off all other things and waited patiently for the maturity of its fruit.

On the other hand, the Tree of Knowledge of Good and Evil continued to have *abundant* fruit on it year-round. Therefore, it was much easier to obtain. The Tree of Knowledge of Good and Evil offered an immediate solution to being made "like God," but without His life and Spirit. This left them with no chance for eternal life. God did not deny the fact that man became like Himself. He declared, "That man indeed has become like one of us, knowing good and evil" (Genesis 3:22, author's paraphrase).

This version of "becoming like one of us" was not what God intended. It was a theological knowing that had no substance of life, a mere form, an empty shell! Isn't that human nature, though, to take the first thing we see as God, and run with it without question? Without waiting and inquiring as to what the true meaning of His full provision is that He has provided? A *proper meaning* attached to things in God is vitally important for our growth. When we don't have this, we accept wrong ideas as right and proceed to make wrong choices, leading us into error as well as leading others with us. Do you realize that because of Adam and Eve's decision to act on knowledge that was partially right, they occasioned the death of themselves, the entire human race, and the Son of God? How many people are dying because of the "version" we have accepted as truth?

There is a widespread weakness in the church and a lack of demonstration of the Spirit in "greater works." To understand this problem we need to dissect the true meaning from that which is false. Let's consider the common phrase used in the church today, "the baptism in the Holy Spirit with the evidence of speaking in tongues."

First of all this is a man-made expression, and nowhere is this found in Scripture. It has been incredibly presumptuous to put these together and form doctrine out of it. Furthermore, it is foolhardy to be banking all our trust on tongues as *the* evidence, while remaining ignorant to the *purpose* and *conditions* for receiving the *Holy Spirit*. If we don't know what we are looking for and why, because the authentic meaning is lost, we will get what we think we should expect and nothing more; but not what we *should* have expected as illustrated at the beginning of this chapter with apples and peaches.

We cannot rightly divide the truth unless the baptism in the Holy Spirit and the evidence of speaking in tongues are separated into two distinct parts. We must, therefore, come to know the true meaning of each, so that the mystery of God's wisdom is revealed for both. This book is dedicated to unfolding the authenticity of the baptism in the Holy Spirit. So let's put our attention towards the true purpose and meaning God intended for "speaking in tongues *as the Spirit gave them utterance.*"

First, understand the meaning of "the Spirit gave them utterance." God was proclaiming that the total control of the believer's will was given over to Him by the Holy Spirit. The Holy Spirit spoke according to God's sovereign will using the faculties of the believer without any interference by the believer at all. Think of this as being "caught up" in God's glory and the Holy Spirit clothing Himself with your vessel, and speaking the oracles of God through you (not that you are completely oblivious to your senses, although this could be the case). Therefore, when the Spirit ceased to give utterance the vessel ceased speaking.

In Gerald Derstine and Joanne Derstine's book, *Following the Fire*, a young man by the name of Amos had a message given through him by God about the end-time revival. The Lord took control over him and the message concluded with: "This is not Amos speaking to you. This is Amos's body you see and Amos's voice you hear, but this is from the Lord your God!" After this his body collapsed into a chair. This was as much the Spirit giving utterance in the English tongue to

English-speaking people as to any other tongue of people in their own language. The point is that the person could not again reproduce what was done through them because it was not within their own power to do so in the first place.

Here is a simple illustration of this: you are standing in front of a group of people and from behind you a loudspeaker booms "Repent, for the kingdom of God is at hand." If someone asked if you could reproduce what happened you could not, because it was out of your control. The only difference between this example and the Spirit giving utterance through you is that you become the loud speaker.

What has been largely received as tongues in the church is the *gift of tongues,* given to be under the control of the believer's will. Therefore, this cannot be confused with God *superseding* your own natural power and speaking through you. This is what "the Spirit gave them utterance" means. It's supernatural and beyond you.

The method by which *tongues* are received in the church today is completely under the charge of the person and is consequently willed by the person, having complete control over his or her own faculties, to continue or cease, as any of the other gifts. For example, Paul exhorts believers to practice prophesying. To do this it must be under the control of the believer *to practice* this. The same is true with wisdom, if you cease to think about the things of God, no new revelation comes and wisdom is stopped. I don't suggest that *tongues* are of a natural origin, just as *prophecy* or *wisdom* is not of a natural origin. Therefore, the argument is not whether the *gift* is from God, but that the gift is under the will of the individual.

Therefore, your will, not just your mouthpiece, must be under the direct control of the Holy Spirit to speak in tongues as He gives the utterance.

When the Lord poured out His Spirit on the day of Pentecost, for the first time since the creation of man, God was given *total control* over man's will. This was the first thing God was declaring by this outpouring. This is incredibly important to understand with all clarity. Now let's move on to the second, broader reason *why* the Lord purposed to give utterance through man by His Spirit.

The Bible states that two or three witnesses shall establish the matter. This is a principle used in the Bible and by God to validate truth. The two scriptural witnesses of *"the Spirit gave them utterance"* that are used today center on the Upper Room at Pentecost and Cornelius's house. Although these two accounts hold similar content to the event of receiving the Holy Spirit, they in no wise give evidence to what the baptism is to an individual inwardly and what the outcome of that is outwardly.

God had a specific purpose for these two accounts accompanied by speaking in tongues as the Spirit gave utterance in Scripture. They were to be the sign that marked the two distinct births of the church, the Jews first and then the Gentiles. These births were as the "star of Bethlehem" was for Jesus. Jupiter (considered the Father planet in the ancient world) and Venus (the mother) passed so close to each other that it created a very bright "star" in the sky. The church, being made up of two peoples, came together to form the fullness of Christ's glory!

> For to make in himself of twain one new man, so making peace; and that He might reconcile both unto God in one body by the cross.
>
> —EPHESIANS 2:15–16

Let's look at the first birthing of the Jewish church and fully understand how to appropriate this event of speaking in tongues as an evidence for God's universal purpose in the earth.

> And they were all filled with the Holy Ghost, and began to speak with other tongues, as the Spirit gave them utterance.
> —ACTS 2:4

Then in verses 7–8 it says:

> And they were all amazed and marvelled, saying one to another, Behold, are not all these which speak Galileans? And how hear we every man in our own tongue, wherein we were born?

Peter stood with the eleven and addressed the people. Now notice the progression starting at vv.14, 22 and 36.

> Ye men of *Judaea*, and all *ye that dwell at Jerusalem...* (emphasis added).

> Ye men of *Israel*, hear these words...(emphasis added).

> Therefore let *all the house of Israel* know assuredly, that God hath made that same Jesus, whom ye have crucified both Lord and Christ (emphasis added).

Peter made the address locally, then regionally, than to the uttermost parts of the earth, encompassing all Israelites everywhere. Pentecost was one of the yearly feasts that all Israelite males were required to attend. Therefore, every male Israelite from the "uttermost parts of the earth" would have been there!

Now look at how many regional languages are mentioned in Acts 2:9–11:

1. Parthians

2. Medes

3. Elamites

4. dwellers in Mesopotamia

5. Judaea

6. Cappadocia

7. Pontus

8. Asia

9. Phrygia

10. Pamphylia

11. the parts of Libya about Cyrene

12. strangers of Rome, Jews and proselytes

13. Cretes

14. Arabians

Since the Bible tells us that the people said "their own language" and "their own tongue" in verses 6 and 8 this naturally means that the language in which they were born was their first language. So, either these people did not understand Hebrew at all or if they did, hearing it in the Galilean accent would have been difficult to understand at best.

Therefore, Peter would have addressed the local and regional Jews of Judea in the Hebrew tongue, while the other disciples standing with him interpreted for every other region in their own language, according to the nations represented there. Otherwise how else would they hear the message in unison clearly and concisely? Verse 37 tells us "*When they heard this*"; who were they? *All of the people*, which provoked the question "*Men and brethren, what shall we do?*" The divine order by which this miraculous sign was brought forth could have only been done under the direct control of the Holy Spirit. What was the result?

> Then they that gladly received *his word* were baptized, and the same day there were added unto them about three thousand souls.
>
> —ACTS 2:41, EMPHASIS ADDED

Whose word was it? It was Peter's word and all could understand because they heard *his word* in their own language!

Speaking in other tongues, as the Spirit gave them utterance on the day of Pentecost, was clearly for the *birthing of the Jewish church.*

Let's look at the events that took place around Cornelius's house, which was the second birthing, the birth of the Gentile church.

As Cornelius prayed an angel came and told him to call for Peter. (See Acts 10:1–8.) When Peter came he called together his kinsmen and near friends. Then Scripture tells us in Acts 10:44–46:

While Peter yet spake these words, the Holy Ghost fell on all them which heard the word. And they of the circumcision which believed were astonished, as many as came with Peter, because that on the Gentiles also was poured out the gift of the Holy Ghost. For they heard them speak with tongues, and magnify God.

Now we see that they of the circumcision which believed were astonished, as many as came with Peter. Why? Because the Holy Spirit came and they heard them speak with tongues and magnify God. Hearing them "magnify God" is the key to our understanding. If the Gentiles were speaking in an unknown language how would those of the circumcision have *known* they were magnifying God? They must have been speaking fluently in the Jewish dialect for the Jews to claim this. It had to be understandable to the Jewish ear.

Listen to what Paul says in 1 Corinthians 14:2:

For he that speaketh in an *unknown* tongue speaketh not unto men, but unto God: for *no man understandeth* him; howbeit in the Spirit he speaketh mysteries (emphasis added).

This unknown tongue that Paul is talking about here is the *gift of tongues*, followed up by Paul from the twelfth chapter of Corinthians, which can't possibly be what we are dealing with at Cornelius's house. In fact it is quite plausible that the Gentiles were quoting sacred texts from God's Word that would only be known and understood by their Jewish audience, thus producing the reaction of "astonishment"!

Why did God do this? Clearly the Lord wanted something to be understood by the Jews. Therefore he sent an infallible proof as a sign to make it plain to the believing Jews His purpose, here and at Pentecost. Therefore, God used language full circle. The Jews spoke to all other Jews in their foreign tongues, now the Gentiles were fulfilling prophecy and speaking back to the Jews.

> For with stammering lips and another tongue will He
> speak to this people!
>
> —ISAIAH 28:11

> In the law it is written, with men of other tongues will I
> speak unto this people; and yet for all that will they not
> hear me, saith the Lord. Wherefore *tongues are for a sign.*
>
> —1 CORINTHIANS 14:21–22, EMPHASIS ADDED

(We will pick this up again and look at what Paul is saying more closely in a moment.)

The Scripture doesn't stop here though; the entire matter is rehearsed in the ears of the rest of the believing Jews at Jerusalem in Acts 11:1–18. This is also so we can clearly see the picture that God wants us to see. So Peter says in verses 15–18:

> And as I began to speak, the Holy Ghost fell on them *as
> on us at the beginning.* Then remembered I the word of the
> Lord, how that He said, John indeed baptized with water;
> but ye shall be baptized with the Holy Ghost. Forasmuch
> then as God gave them the like gift as he did unto us, who
> believed on the Lord Jesus Christ; what was I, that I could
> withstand God? When they [the Jews] *heard these things,*
> they held their peace, and *glorified God, saying, then,*
> hath God *also to the Gentiles granted repentance unto life*
> (emphasis added).

Do you see? God duplicated the first experience so the *Jewish church* would be forced to acknowledge that this was the "*birth*" of the Gentile church; hence, the words, "*fell on them, as on us,*" and "*what was I, that I could withstand God,*" and "*when they heard these things.*" This was the sign for the Jews that marked the beginning of Christ's church as one unified body!

Peter and the others needed this kind of proof because in Acts 10:28 he says:

Ye know how that it is an unlawful thing for a man that
is a Jew to keep company, or come unto one of another
nation; but God hath [shown] me I should not call any man
common or unclean (emphasis added).

God brought Peter and the others this far by the vision Peter had
seen in Acts 10:11–16, but this teaching of not keeping company with
one of another nation was ingrained in them. It was so ingrained that
even Paul had to rebuke Peter for distancing himself from the Gentiles
later on! (See Galatians 2:11–14.) These Jews needed *astonishing evidence*
to accept the Gentiles into the fold. None of them believed that there
would be a Gentile church made up of the uncircumcised! The Jews
had to see the sign before they could accept that God would grant the
Gentiles repentance unto life.

Consider Acts 8:15–17, when Peter and John went down to pray that
the Samaritans would receive the Holy Spirit; the Jews didn't need
"astonishing evidence," therefore there is no mention of tongues. It
was simply a matter of fact thing; the apostles prayed and the people
of Samaria received; end of the story.

From these two major events in Scripture we see that this is the
appropriate application for speaking in tongues as *"an evidence."*
It built the validity of the two distinct churches, forming one body.
This evidence stood up as if in "a court of law" convincing the Jewish
believers, and proved to every Gentile that they had been grafted into
the olive tree beyond a shadow of a doubt. We can understand why
Christ said to Peter:

Upon this rock I will build My *church*; and the gates of hell
shall not prevail against it.

—MATTHEW 16:18, EMPHASIS ADDED

It was Peter who laid the first stone for each church through God's
sign, that birthed both the Jewish church and the Gentile church, and
the gates of hell indeed did not prevail against it! The building had
begun!! For further proof we return to what Paul says and read:

> In the law it is written, With men of other tongues will I speak unto this people; and yet for all that will they not hear me, saith the Lord. Wherefore *tongues are for a sign,* not to them that believe, but *to them that believe not.*
>
> —1 CORINTHIANS 14:21–22, EMPHASIS ADDED

The Lord is not talking about a strange speech or hard language, "*whose words thou canst not understand*" (Ezek. 3:6), for a sign, but a coherent language understood by the hearers. On the day of Pentecost and at Cornelius's house God used this sign for its intended function, the birthings of the church. There was another very important reason for this sign, which is behind all of God's doings: to do what He really enjoys, by fulfilling His own words; fulfilling prophecy, bringing to pass what was spoken centuries before, to establish in all minds His absolute control and dominion! Let's look at what Paul goes on to say in 1 Corinthians 14:23, and be aware of the important distinction he is making:

> If therefore the whole church be come together into one place, and all speak with tongues, and there come in those that are unlearned, or unbelievers [*"those that believe not,"* v.22], *will they not say that ye are mad?* (emphasis added).

Wait a minute, Paul just said tongues were for a sign to "those that believe not." It seems from one verse to the next Paul has contradicted himself. But in fact he has not; Paul is making a distinction between tongues as a sign and tongues as a gift in the church *for edification.* Therefore, he goes on to exhort the believers in verses 27–28:

> If any man speak in an *unknown tongue,* [which is what he is implying in v.23] let it be by two, or at the most by three, and that by course [or, "in order"]; and let one interpret. But if there *be no interpreter, let him keep silence* in the church; and let him speak to himself, and to God (emphasis added).

This is the gift of tongues given to the church, which speaks mysteries to God, but not the "sign of tongues," which is *coherent* language that had birthed the church. *All the Jews* would have known the Old Testament scripture spoken by Paul in verse 21. They would have understood the specific purpose for this "sign," and could see God's unmistakable hand in it. The sign was for the Jews. At Pentecost and Cornelius's house the Jews would have known immediately by the Scriptures this indeed is God. It was this strong evidence for them that fulfilled God's written Word!

Look back at Peter's choice of Scripture he uses to address the circumcision on Pentecost in Acts 2:16–20. Twice it says, "I will pour out my Spirit" and twice "they shall prophecy"; once referring to "visions" and once to "dreams," but no mention of tongues. Why? The Jews could make the connection from Scripture and by the witness that they saw that this was the Holy Spirit's outpouring, but proclaimed in *each of their own languages*. This was the evidence they needed; God hit the intended mark.

> There is neither Greek nor Jew, circumcision nor uncircumcision.
>
> —COLOSSIANS 3:11

We can conclude that God was *not establishing tongues* as evidence to prove that this was the Holy Spirit's coming, but as the sign that established the *beginning of the church*!

"The evidence" is that the presence of the Holy Spirit was in the tabernacle of mankind to dwell forever, and *what* that meant for the individual was *much* more than the sign of tongues God was using to birth the two olive trees and the two candlesticks (Rev. 11:4). As significant as this sign was for its intended purpose, the Gentile church today has misunderstood it and has sought after this sign to represent something that it was never meant to be.

Therefore let us also consider another very important detail. Neither the Jews nor the Gentiles in either incident had any preconceived ideas of what speaking in tongues was. This came as a *total surprise without any warning*. When the Holy Spirit came and performed His work through them in the language of man, the early disciples could say, "Oh, where did that come from?" But now the reverse is taking place; tongues and *any kind of tongues* for that matter is what is looked for; and then considered to be the Holy Spirit.

This is like saying, "my friend is here in my house because his coat is hanging on the hook," when he is actually at his place of work! Hence, this kind of thinking defies any kind of logic. The method which the body uses to propagate the baptism in the Holy Spirit is flawed and not biblical! The apostles after the event of Pentecost never taught for anyone to open their mouth and let whatever comes out, come out. Nor did they put any *preconceived ideas* into people's minds about what they should expect. This method, therefore, falls under the law of suggestion that is under the direct control of man. We have sold the gift of the Holy Spirit and His purpose through lack of knowledge, ignorance, and pride for something immediate, as Adam and Eve did. Remember Proverbs 25:2:

> It is the glory of God to conceal a thing: but the honour of kings is to search out a matter.

Don't just take what is on the menu. This is God's precious pearl of *great* price, the same Spirit that raised Jesus from the dead, and must be *understood* with all wisdom. We must draw clear lines between tongues as a "first-fruits" gift, tongues as a "sign," and what the gift of the Holy Spirit really is. The loss of the true understanding of the Holy Spirit baptism is the greatest tragedy in the history of the church. We have put God in a box with our own interpretation on it and have become the masters of our own delusion.

If there is any misunderstanding, let me interject here by reassuring my reader that I hold all the gifts in high regard. As Paul says, covet earnestly the best gifts (1 Cor. 12:31), and this includes tongues. Tongues are not "evil" as some might suppose I am saying, they are languages of heavenly origin and have their proper place. But when tongues is applied to mean more than it is meant to or when it was not within the same context scripturally, then to correct that ideology may come across as negative.

Therefore, ask yourself, was your experience heaven sent? Was it completely out of your control? Did it take you by surprise? God is a God of surprise for the very purpose that He gets the glory! This element of surprise seems to mark the majority of testimonies of people who sought God directly for the baptism; waiting, some for months or even years, not knowing the day or the hour. Again, are you fulfilling the "greater works" of Jesus? Is the church at large fulfilling them?

Consider this question, if we know now that tongues as the *Spirit gave utterance* was the avenue God used to birth the church, why would He need to use the same method after the church has been born? The answer is simple, He doesn't; but our human nature feels that it needs to control God's workings (maybe so things remain civilized), ties His hands and demands that this is the way it has got to be done. All the while God is actually saying I will give you what you need to fulfill your purpose when the Holy Spirit comes to dwell in you.

Think about it, are you going to address one hundred thousand people of a different language when He comes? Maybe you will; if so He will equip you for it. But if not, what purpose does it serve at the immediate reception of His coming? You need to get your mind off any preconceived ideas. He is the Lord and He will give you what you need, and you take what He gives you.

Think. Your purpose in the earth and what you need are *unique to you*. The important thing that you need to know is the person of the Holy Spirit, what His function is when He comes into your life, and that He will decide what your inward and outward testimony will be at His initial reception. When you understand and accept this, tongues is laid to rest, because it is not the essence of the matter at all. Consider that Rees Howells, Maria Woodworth-Etter, Charles Finney, and Dwight L. Moody all received baptisms in the Holy Spirit without mentioning speaking in tongues as a gift or as the Spirit gives utterance. The use of tongues may have been manifested later in their lives, but it is not reported at the Holy Spirit's initial reception (if they did this was not the emphasis), because tongues are not the issue. What they all do testify to is far beyond what is testified to today; their experiences were genuine, producing the *outworking evidence.* Man has made tongues the defining issue for the baptism. Therefore the church remains in sickness, and darkness without the dominion prescribed to us in the pages of the Bible; leaving us hungering for more because we are not satisfied, when Jesus Himself said, drink from these waters and you will *never thirst again.* Let us humble ourselves and look at what our eyes really need to be on: Him!

Chapter 3

JUSTIFICATION: COVERING VS. CHANGE

THERE WAS A certain man accused of a crime, ready to be sentenced before a judge. An honorable man stepped forward and said, "Take my life to bear the sentence that is to be appointed to him by the court and let this man go free." The judge agrees and hands out the sentence for the crime, which the honorable man carries out, while the criminal goes free.

The criminal therefore was justified or made blameless in the eyes of the court. Nevertheless, was this criminal changed by the benevolent act of the honorable man? Was his environment changed? Did his personality or behavior change? Did the incident erase the fact that it really was him that committed the crime? Would he not bear the same name to which he was born? Would not all things remain the same before and after he entered the courtroom? This man indeed remained the same throughout the exchange the honorable man provided. The type of person he was and had become, shaped by his environment and innate personality from childhood to adulthood, didn't change. The only thing that may have changed is the positive effect of the benevolent act on the criminal's heart and mind; to a larger or lesser degree depending on the hardness of heart. Those who are forgiven little, love little, those who are forgiven much, love much. Therefore, this could only prompt the criminal to change his behavior in a natural way, "turning over a new leaf" as one might say. In the biblical sense it would be repentance.

This is an illustration of what Jesus Christ did for us on the cross. He fulfilled the sentence that was meant for us. What was the sentence? Death. Sin requires a sentence of death, therefore we were required to pay with our very life, and the life of a person is in the blood. Therefore the Lord gave His own life and blood on the cross to set us free from the judgment against us. But the Lord's blood, which opened the door for our justification, was never meant to be the totality of our experience. In all that Christ has accomplished, our growth has become stunted because most of us have put all of our weight on justification and stopped.

This is where the deception runs deep enough to put people in a complacent state, being thankful they are not going to hell and living out their natural lives till they die and go to heaven. It is true, just as the criminal could be moved to change his behavior because of the benevolent act of the honorable man, we likewise are moved positively in our behavior when our eyes are opened spiritually; seeing the criminal acts we have committed against God and that Christ as Savior took our place that was meant for us. By Jesus's act we were made blameless in the sight of God, having our sins covered by His blood; this is what justification is.

But let us truly understand the depth of justification. As the aspects of the criminal's life didn't change when he was dismissed from the charges, neither does our life. Why? It is because the event was factual in nature as any other event in history. Therefore, the benevolent act itself and what it means proves to be the *positive effect* on the person's heart and mind. This is true for the believer as well. We enter into the Christian life by what is historically factual; simply being that Christ died and shed His blood to justify us before God. We understand with our minds, and believe in our hearts that this is the truth. It is obvious to note that this does require the drawing of the Father by the Holy Spirit; bringing knowledge of guilt and conviction for the charges laid against us; helping us to see our need to accept by faith the factual events of Christ's sacrifice. These things are of a spiritual nature and need to be spiritually discerned; therefore, God's Spirit aids us in this process.

The positive effect on our heart and mind in seeing the historical significance of Christ's sacrifice in relation to our own lives, allows the Holy Spirit to give us a measure of repentance according to the hardness of our heart. In other words, to what degree the act of Christ's sacrifice positively affected our heart and mind, determines how much softening and opening of the heart takes place; in turn receiving the measure of repentance equivalent to it. This is why preachers (for example Charles Finney) who have the anointing to bring strong conviction upon the people see more lasting and fruitful conversions. Furthermore, to what degree repentance is received to the making of our wrongs right, past and present towards God and man, is equivalent to the positive effect it has on our outward behavior. But even though we accepted Christ's sacrifice and became justified, and our outward behavior may have changed, everything else remains the same, just as it was for the criminal in the example.

For the believer, we need to understand what has not changed, spiritually speaking. Being justified did not remove the devil from our lives. He still knows us as before and torments us as he always did. Nor has justification removed our inbred sin or the sin nature. Nor has it removed the susceptibility of sickness and disease. This is proved by the very lives that make up Christ's body. Think of your own life, when you were justified by accepting the blood of Christ. After the glow of having your eyes opened to Christ's sacrifice and a change through repentance took place, did you still recognize that anger from your father in your life? Or the controlling nature that was upon your mother residing in you? Or maybe it was the intense irrational fear that came down from your grandmother, or the impatience that came from another in your family line still living through you. Had doctors told you that you may develop a disease your mother or father had, and then it happened? Or did you just fall prey to sickness in your life? What about inbred sin? Did you discover another law in your members waging war against you? Had you been overtaken by lust or covetousness when you really wanted to do what God wants? Paul is obviously referring to a believer who is struggling with this kind of defeat in Romans chapter 7.

If we are honest, we will all agree that we have experienced defeat in our lives at some point *after* justification has taken place. There is no reason to be ashamed if we have a pure heart and really want to please God. It is only that our ignorance must be enlightened through understanding to move on. The real problem of course is man's pride against acknowledging the defeat; sweeping these issues under the carpet and avoiding looking at them, let alone talking about them.

Justification was never meant to be an antidote for everything in the believer's life. For example, the sick of the palsy was lowered down from the roof and Jesus said, "Thy sins be forgiven thee." Jesus justified the man but the man's condition was not changed. The man's healing and being made whole was a separate grace apart from justification. In fact his healing was the proof of the man's justification to the onlookers. Deathbed repentance is another example; people accept Christ's sacrifice near the end of their lives and die with the conditions of their life and circumstances remaining the same. Some may receive healing and be raised up, but what I'm getting at is we haven't stopped "being" sinners at our *core*, even though we have been justified.

The Lord laid down His life and shed His blood for God first and the outcome for mankind was second. It was the Father's will that Christ shed His blood. It was the reason He gave His only begotten Son. The Father brought before His own altar a spotless Lamb chosen from the foundation of the world, to make atonement for Adam's sin and all mankind. The sacrifice was to appease the Father's heart, to satisfy His own wrath and remove the judgment of man from off His mind to an appointed day. We benefited by being put in a different perspective in the Father's eyes. It was God's command in the Old Testament that an animal give his life and blood for sin. God demanded this; man does not demand this, but God does. He wanted to look upon man without sin and this was the only way He could. But God went a step further and prepared another human life as the ultimate sacrifice to lay to rest the justice required against sin. Therefore, Christ's sacrifice was perfect, spotless and without blemish, which we will discover in greater detail later.

God required sacrifice so He could remain a righteous judge in holiness and be forgiving at the same time. For this reason we can stand in God's court blameless, justified, and through the blood of Christ He can look upon us without seeing sin so long as we are faithful. You need to understand this point. You didn't change (other than how I specified earlier) on the whole as an individual in regard to your inheritance of inward sin. You only stand in a different position before God, because He now *sees* you *differently.*

As in the Old Testament and in the New, the blood provides a covering over man from God's judgment. Therefore, this segment of the Lord's life has not touched and changed the fallen nature of man directly. The Lord's blood was pointed heavenward for the purpose and function it was intended for. The Lord shows us the function of the blood first introduced at the Passover in Egypt. These things are all types and shadows of things to come. We can clearly see the purpose here laid out by God when the Israelites put the blood around the door; God saw the blood as a barrier between His judgment and man and passed over that house. The blood itself did not change the Israelites' lives within themselves. The blood saved the people from the sentence of death, which was an actual outward event, producing celebration and thankfulness in the hearts of the people, just as it has for all those who have accepted Christ's blood as their barrier between themselves and God's judgment of eternal damnation. Nevertheless, it didn't switch the Israelites from being a self-willed, complaining, and a fearful company of people within. Their carnal nature continued to be in enmity against God.

Jesus's sacrifice was better in that it removed the dead works of ordinances of animal sacrifice, (Heb. 10:9) establishing His own blood to be received by faith. Also, His atonement is timeless, stretching from the foundation of the world to the end of time. But the function and purpose for the blood does remain consistent with teachings of the Old Testament, that of covering.

For example, if you were drowning in a sea of water, the sea of water being God's judgment, and a rubber lifeboat floats to your aid, by climbing into it you are now floating above the water. Between you and the sea is a thin layer of rubber that has separated you from death. You were the *same* in the water and out of the water. The blood of Christ is like that thin layer of rubber separating man from death, but man's fallen nature was untouched the moment after Jesus shed His blood and gave up the ghost, remaining as it was before.

The dynamics of Heaven changed; the ordinances on earth changed.

The position man had towards God and God towards man changed. A great many things changed but the corruption within man did not. Why? The blood alone was not given to produce such a change! Blood is directly correlated with *judgment and the establishing of covenants.* Therefore, blood was shed to establish the agreement that man's sins would be covered and judgment would be passed over. So when Scriptures tell us that we are washed in the Lord's blood for the forgiveness of our sins, (if we have accepted Christ and are faithful to Him) we have been washed from God's judgment. But this is a change in our position in God's relation towards us and cannot be confused with our corrupt nature remaining the same.

We see this fact in the lives of the disciples even after Jesus rose from the dead. None of them believed, they were all living in fear and doubt; their minds were darkened from the Scriptures and still stayed on carnal matters. All of these things are born out of man's fallen nature. Nevertheless, these people were justified. They believed in Christ, yet from looking at their lives you cannot tell when they were justified because it wasn't within them to produce that evidence. They stayed the same, but *God's relationship towards them changed,* and that is what created their justification. Jesus declared, "It is finished," not because man changed but because God's conditions were met to justify man. This is not complete salvation in the mind of God. Jesus's blood is only the surface of what He achieved for mankind. This is only the first part, the gateway to man's total redemption. But what has this accomplished for man?

> In whom we have *boldness* and *access* with *confidence* by the faith of Him.
> —EPHESIANS 3:12, EMPHASIS ADDED

> Having therefore, brethren, *boldness* to enter into the holiest by the blood of Jesus.
> —HEBREWS 10:19, EMPHASIS ADDED

God can look upon us as covered and we can approach Him in prayer and seek Him for His complete salvation boldly with confidence. According to what Jesus accomplished in totality, having been established in the mind of God for man, He can hear our prayer and answer us. If you have built your entire Christian life on this one aspect (justification) of Christ's life alone, whether you have been in the "church" for years or in some sort of "service" for decades, you are remaining in the elementary stage of the life that Christ provided.

Unfortunately, justification has been interpreted to mean total salvation over the years. But justification is only one part of salvation, and we are in danger when we lump it as the whole. Without clear definitions, which create definite markers to point the way, the body as a result is suffering from leanness and weakness. Taking the example from the previous chapter, peaches have become apples. When the definition loses its true meaning or you think it means more than it does, you have just been led to believe that a *fraction* is the whole. This could ruin the potential in anyone spiritually, setting a limitation leading to a stunting of growth.

A simple illustration would be a potted plant. The pot is justification, and you are the plant. The plant has been led to believe that when it reaches the outer limits and becomes root-bound it stops growing and succumbs to its borders. The plant doesn't realize, because of misunderstanding, that full salvation is found in the earth outside, where there is no limit of soil, beyond the pot of justification.

You may say, "I have experienced this or that in God, I have received healing from this or that, or I have received this gift from God and operate in it." I say wonderful, God is loving and gracious and we all need to grow from some point. But here are some questions to see what stage you are at in the Lord's plan of salvation. Do you still live according to your fallen nature? Are there still things in your life you are powerless to overcome? Does sin still lie at your door? Are you just as fearful and unbelieving as you were before you accepted Christ? Are you still a friend of the world? Do you live your life for yourself to fit into society as one living the "normal" Christian life? Is your life fruitless and barren? Does your fruit remain untarnished? Are you living a life of sickness and disease? Is the devil more of an overcomer in your life than you are? Do you find it easier to put your trust in doctors, counselors, medicines, and drugs than in the living God?

The list could go on, but anyone who can understand and humble himself and see the trend of defeat and failure can add himself to the list. I do not write this to condemn anyone, but to draw your attention to something amiss. Justification is the beginning of the believer's life. Here we can press God for His precious promises and experience the full salvation He has in mind for us on earth. Let us fully understand His purpose and move on. There is no reason for defeat when we become enlightened to Christ's total accomplishment and provision for His body.

Chapter 4

THE ISSUE OF SIN

A DISTINCTION MUST BE made here between a lifestyle of sin (whether premeditated or in ignorance) vs. inherited sin so there is no confusion. Before a person is converted in his *heart* to Christ, he lives his life as he pleases. He has no acknowledgment that anything he does is sinful in nature and against God. Upon true conversion to Christ however, God grants people new eyes to see their behavior. They see the sinful, selfish life they have been living and the consequences of that lifestyle brought to themselves and others, as shown forth in the previous chapter. Thus, God removes the ignorance from their minds and they "know" their actions, which in turn motivates them to repent and change outwardly. When repentance takes place, God is merciful and faithful through Christ to forgive us because these things were done in ignorance.

> ...but I obtained mercy, because I did it ignorantly in my unbelief.
>
> —1 Timothy 1:13

But as Hebrews 10:26 tells us,

> For if we sin willfully after that we have received the knowledge of the truth, there remaineth no more sacrifice for sins.

That is to say, if you're deliberately going against the knowledge of the truth and your conscience, doing things that are sinful and not pleasing to God, there remains no sacrifice. Therefore, God holds us *responsible* for sinful behavior that *we can control* by His grace. For example, we can remove ourselves from wicked company, and stop going to establishments that perpetrate sin because it is under our control to do so. If our conversion is genuine then we naturally change our minds about our previous way of life and no longer desire the things we once took pleasure in. Furthermore, the Holy Spirit resurrects our conscience and it becomes alive to God, convicting us of things we have done in our past and present.

Let us now turn our focus to inherited sin. This is sin that no matter what we do it has the mastery over us and we are indeed slaves to it. Paul illustrated this perfectly in Romans 7:14–25; in verse 23 he says:

> ...bringing me into captivity to the law of sin which is in my members.

God is responsible for removing sin that is within us which is *beyond* our control. God expects us to do our part, under our control, and as we seek Him, He will remove what we cannot. This is an established principle in Scripture; our duty, then His.

> Draw near to God and He will draw near to you.
>
> —JAMES 4:8, NKJV

I believe this is where the body of Christ has been robbed of knowledge and lied to. In knowledge, because even if we had a deep conversion in our heart and mind there is no true understanding of what we are expected to do or become. In lies because we have been told we are sinners saved by grace, and that justification encompasses everything and that's all. That only takes us up half the mountain but not to the peak. If we know what we are responsible for and do it, and *see the whole truth* of what God purposes to do, we would seek Him to become sinless saints, perfect as He is perfect, holy as He is Holy, destined to be the Lamb's wife.

So how does God deal with inherited sin? In two ways; we will look at the first way now and cover the second way in the following chapter. From the Old Testament we can see that when an animal was given for a sin offering the blood made the atonement or covering for the sin in the eyes of God. When the sacrifice was made, a divine transfer was made. The person's sin transferred into and upon the animal. The animal was given the sin *in place* of the person, thus the atonement was made. Nevertheless, there is a deeper meaning regarding the animal that the Lord wants us to know.

The priest would take a few specific inward parts of the animal and burn them on the altar as a sin offering before the Lord. The rest of the remaining carcass would be burnt with fire outside the camp. This is important to be able to follow the connection. Everything that was in the person that defiled him in God's eyes would be transferred to the animal and because of that the person would go free. The very life required for justice, the animal provided; the very sin to be destroyed by fire upon the altar, the animal provided; and the very nature of sin that *caused* the sin to be burnt without the camp the animal also provided.

God is showing man that the nature of sin is so rooted in us that if we were to pay for our own sin, it would require our very life and our body burnt to ashes! Now see the symbolism here. Jesus was the last Lamb to be sacrificed.

> The bodies of those beasts, whose blood is brought into the sanctuary by the high priest for sin, are burned without the camp. Wherefore Jesus also, that He might sanctify the people with His own blood, suffered without the gate.
> —Hebrews 13:11–12

The Lord was given the sin of mankind to bear and Jesus gave His life for God's justice; He did all this outside the gate. Why? Because the animal *carcass* under the first covenant bore the nature of sin, being the root cause of sin in man, which defiles him perpetually, was destroyed by fire outside the camp. This is why God makes specific reference to the remaining carcass of the sin offering.

> And the skin of the bullock, and all his flesh, with his head, and with his legs, and his inwards, and his dung, even the whole bullock shall he carry forth without the camp unto a

clean place, where the ashes are poured out, and burn him
on the wood with fire.

—LEVITICUS 4:11–12

God lists the skin, the flesh, and the inward parts because that is
where the nature of sin is embedded in us and says "even the *whole*
bullock" referring to the total depravity of man. And He specifically
points out his *dung* to be burned which is the *perpetual* defilement
of man. This is why Jesus makes the point in Mark 7:19–20 (author's
paraphrase), "Look boys, we're not dealing with food that turns into
dung being the defiling thing here, but that which comes out of a
man is the defiling dung." By law this defiling nature was to be *burnt*!
So why, if Jesus was paying the whole price for man, was His body
not required to be burnt? From God's perspective it would be unjust
since the body of the Lord was sinless and not defiled with the corrupt
nature of man (which we will look into later). So why exactly did the
Lord suffer without the gate? The Lord God Almighty was declaring
that He was making provision to deal with this corrupt nature that has
defiled mankind; but not at the cross (the cross being our justification).

God sets out to show us in the Old Testament that fire destroys sin,
the origin of sin, uncleanness and anything that defiles. Fire is the only
element established by the Lord that sanctifies and cleanses. He confirms this by commanding:

The fire shall ever be burning upon the altar; it shall never
go out.

—LEVITICUS 6:13

The fire shall continue, ready to destroy all to do with sin. This is
why the second annihilation of all that is wicked on the earth will be
burnt with a fervent heat. Look at 2 Peter 3:12. The first annihilation
we know was the flood, which was symbolic of the waters of baptism,
(1 Pet. 3:20–21) which brought us grace, but fire dissolves everything, it
makes a complete end.

Although the animal sacrifice satisfied God's justice at the time, the
work within man remained incomplete. The man or woman went away

acquitted; yet *unchanged*. Man would continue to remain unchanged inside till God could provide a way to destroy man's sin and the nature of sin in man by fire, without reducing the person to ashes! The Lord gives us a clear illustration of this in the story of Shadrach, Meshach and Abed-nego in the fiery furnace. These three men were justified before God. They were blameless in His sight in regards to the charges laid against them by Nebuchadnezzar. Nevertheless, they were thrown into the fire (Dan. 3:23), but the fire did not hurt them. In verse 27 we're given this record that all the king's men:

> Saw these men, upon whose bodies the fire had no power, nor was an hair of their head singed, neither were their coats changed, nor the smell of fire had passed onto their clothing.
>
> —DANIEL 3:27

Do you understand? God was revealing an ancient secret, that when He sends His fire upon man it shall have no power over their physical bodies, it won't touch a hair or their clothing and they won't even smell it, but it will be there. God does not desire a people that are only clean on the outside of the cup and continue to bring their repentance before Him year after year. No. God takes no pleasure in this; He wants to destroy that nature or origin of sin within us altogether! Just as the entire carcass and its dung was burned outside the camp. How was God going to do this without destroying the body? He would accomplish this by transferring the office of High Priest from an earthly natural one to a heavenly spiritual one.

> Seeing then that we have a great high priest, that is passed into the heavens, Jesus the Son of God.
>
> —HEBREWS 4:14

It was the Son of God who became the minister before God's altar of fire in heaven. If we look back to the fiery furnace:

> Lo, I see four men loose, walking in the midst of the fire, and they have no hurt; and the form of the fourth is like the Son of God.
>
> —DANIEL 3:25

I believe right *here* God the Father established the Son to be the minister of His fire, to accomplish in man what was necessary to be destroyed without destroying the individual. Jesus as High Priest in God's heavenly temple (Heb. 8:1–2) could send God's holy fire from His altar into men. It could burn up sin and the nature of sin where it resides within him and anything that defiles him and yet preserve his life. There is a foreshadow of this in the sixth chapter of Isaiah. In verse 1 Isaiah saw the Lord in His temple in heaven. Then in verse 5 he says:

> I am a man of unclean lips, and I dwell in the midst of a people of unclean lips.

In verse 6–7 a seraphim flew to him:

> Having a live coal in his hand, which he had taken with the tongs from off the altar. And he laid it upon my mouth, and said, Lo, this hath touched thy lips; and *thine iniquity is taken away and thy sin purged* (emphasis added).

Fire was taken off the heavenly altar to purify that which was unclean and Isaiah himself was not consumed. Malachi sees this work of Christ in Malachi 3:2–3:

> For He [Christ] is like a refiner's fire, and like fullers' soap…and He shall purify the sons of Levi, and purge them as gold and silver, that they may offer unto the LORD an offering in righteousness.

John the Baptist according to Matthew 3:11 proclaims Jesus not only to be the baptizer of the Holy Spirit, but the baptizer of *fire* also.

Therefore, it is by a *heavenly fire* that man is sanctified and freed from sin. Why is this important? It is important because the Holy Spirit *cannot*, I repeat, cannot dwell where sin is present. Sin must be purged and cleansed in the individual before the Holy Spirit can dwell in them. God doesn't change the order of things from the old to the new covenant; the old acts as a *map* for the new. If we can understand the old we *will* understand the new. Sin cannot dwell in God's presence. If you approached God in the Old Testament with sin you were killed and cut off from the people. The approaching of God that took place under the old covenant was outwardly in nature, but under the new covenant the shift was made to God wanting to approach us, *inwardly*.

This is where great misunderstanding has taken place in our knowledge of what God requires and has purposed. Jesus's blood covers us and our sin like a sheet; that we may approach God outwardly through prayer, seeking Him. Because of the blood He can accept us and hear us. But for God to approach us on the *inside* we need to be more than covered, we need to be sanctified by fire. Being established by God, this is and always will be, the manner in which our inbred sin or sin nature is dealt with. God is a consuming fire (Heb. 12:29), and it is by this fire that sin is annihilated from us. Therefore it is only then that your house is fit for the presence of God to take up residence. (This should not be confused with experiencing the presence of God in worship, or in our devotional time corporately or individually or receiving a witness by God's Spirit, etc. But what must be understood is the dynamic of God's life and presence overcoming and lifting your life into a divine fellowship perpetually.) Jesus says:

> For every one shall be salted with fire, and every sacrifice shall be salted with salt. Salt is good: but if the salt has lost its saltiness, wherewith will ye season it? Have salt in yourselves.
>
> —Mark 9:49–50

Jesus is skillfully weaving fire and salt together to show us God's desire, taking reference from God's command:

> Every oblation [offering] of thy meat offering shalt thou
> season with salt; neither shalt thou suffer the salt of the
> covenant of thy God to be lacking from thy meat offering:
> with all thine offerings thou shalt offer salt.
>
> —LEVITICUS 2:13, EMPHASIS ADDED

Jesus is clearly tying this covenant of salt on meat offerings to us as *living sacrifices* being *salted with fire*. He exhorts us to have salt in ourselves; have fire in ourselves for it shall *not be lacking* in the plan for man. This is a divine experience that must come from off the altar of heaven. Not something conjured up, but a real fire inside. Charles Finney described it as liquid fire. Gerald Derstine in his book, *Following the Fire*, described it as a ball of fire that began to roar in the pit of his stomach and sent its flames up through his body.[1] Stanley Jones declares, "I was filled with a strange refining fire that seemed to course through every portion of my being in cleansing waves. It was all very quiet and I had hold of myself and yet the Divine waves could be felt from the inmost center of my being to my fingertips. My whole being was being fused into one, and through the whole there was a sense of sacredness and awe and the most exquisite joy. John Wesley, the Methodist preferred to call the experience 'perfect love' the very same words 'this is perfect love' spoken by God to Gerald Derstine when this refining fire came upon him. William Booth the Salvationist liked to describe it as 'the blessing of a clean heart.'"[2] This event can be experienced before or simultaneously with the baptism in the Holy Spirit, *but never after*, since the house must be *cleansed first*.

This is true to Scripture. The 120 in the Upper Room were baptized in the baptism of fire signified by the *"cloven tongues like of fire"* that appeared on each one. This visible sign was no mistake and obviously revealed for our understanding as to what God has been foreshadowing. Their sin was destroyed; their lives were cleansed for the Holy Spirit to dwell in them. (Unfortunately, when words like cloven "tongues" are used the mind may immediately think of languages, but in fact it was a word used to describe a flickering flame, which is representing that all consuming fire of the Holy Spirit.) If you search your heart and the understanding of the Scriptures you will know this is God's true desire. The church needs to become fully enlightened on the issues of our sin nature and how God has made provision to adequately deal with it, without falling short.

Consider the outcome of the human race; it is because of sin. Everything that has happened is because of sin. It is of utmost importance that we grasp God's ultimate goal: to fully erase sin that He may commune with man. Think of God's heart. Do you think it satisfies Him to just *look* upon you without sin? No! God wants to be in you without the barrier of sin as a passionate lover for His bride. Make this your heart's cry to be cleansed from the nature of sin and all that defiles you by Jesus's baptism of fire!

Chapter 5

THE ISSUE OF SIN CONTINUED: THE PLAGUE OF LEPROSY

L
ET'S MAKE ANOTHER important connection that God uses to illustrate the nature of sin within us.

> And the leper in whom the plague is, his clothes shall be rent, and his head bare, and he shall put a covering upon his upper lip, and shall cry, Unclean, unclean. All the days wherein the plague shall be in him he shall be defiled; he is unclean: he shall dwell alone; without the camp shall his habitation be.
>
> —LEVITICUS 13:45–46

Leprosy is a plague that is *highly infectious* and symbolic of the sin nature that dwells in man. *It has infected every individual in the human race.*

We must note first that the blood covering was not the order of dealing with the problem of leprosy. The command was *separation.* The person was defiled like the dung of the sacrifice "all the days it was in him" and pronounced unclean. The way the sentence is phrased does suggest that there *could* be days in the future in which the plague is *not* there. Nevertheless, while it was in him he was to dwell alone, *cut off* from "the living population" and from God's sanctuary, left to die without hope.

This is what the sin nature has forced upon us, to die *alone* apart from God's presence. The person was still an Israelite, but where was the person to dwell? Outside the camp! The same place the remains of the animal sacrifice were to be burnt. This is no coincidence but for our understanding. God did not decree that the leper should be burnt, because we are dealing with human life, remember. But we can see that sin has separated man from God, leaving him totally defiled, and that defilement *is to be* cleansed by fire. To further prove this point and complete the connection the Lord uses the word "leprosy" *generically.* Therefore, leprosy means *not only* a human disease but that which may be found in *physical objects.* By doing this God draws out the picture that we are to perceive.

> The garment also that the plague of leprosy is in, whether it be a woolen garment, or a linen garment, whether it be in the warp, or woof; of linen, or of woolen; whether in a skin, or in any thing made of skin.
>
> —LEVITICUS 13:47–48

The priest was to look at it and leave it seven days to see if it would spread. If it did spread:

> The plague is a *fretting* leprosy; it is unclean. He shall therefore *burn* that garment, whether warp or woof, in woollen or in linen, or any thing of skin, wherein the plague is: for it is a fretting leprosy; it shall be *burnt in the fire.*
>
> —LEVITICUS 13:51–52, EMPHASIS ADDED

God uses the word "fretting" to describe what this leprosy does. It devours, wears, corrodes, eats away and destroys. On a personal level, fret can also be described as an irritant or vexation, to grate or agitate.[1] The sin nature is the reality of all these descriptive words, both in action and what it does emotionally. The leprosy that hasn't spread is described as being "*fret inward*" (v. 55) and God declares that *both* kinds of leprosy are unclean, just as He did the leprous person. But in this case God uses the garment *metaphorically* to show how He *truly desires* to deal with this problem. Just as the skin, flesh and the whole carcass including the dung of the sacrifice, God commands the priest to burn the garment with fire. Carrying out these commands was all part of the priests job.

God uses a house as one more example in which leprosy may be found. More specifically in the *walls* of a house, which make up the outer frame of the dwelling. (See Leviticus 14:37.) What is the outer frame of *our* dwelling? Our *bodies*. God makes this interesting statement in Leviticus 14:34:

> *I put* the plague of leprosy in a house (emphasis added).

Why would God create such destruction? So we can see the object lesson. So we *don't miss it*. Let these objects be consumed so we won't be!

Let's summarize where leprosy can be found: in man, in clothing and in houses. God is pointing out very clearly sin in us, sin clothing us, and sin surrounding us. What is God's high calling for us? To cleanse us, clothe us, and inhabit us.

Before we move on I want to note something else God is showing us. At the beginning of the previous chapter I made the distinction between two types of sin: that which is fleshy and outward and that, which is inherited, inward. (We saw those two types being dealt with in the animal sacrifice.) Therefore when God is dealing with leprosy in the *garment* and in *man* there are two washings.

There is a *first* washing (Lev.13:54, 14:8), a *waiting period*, then a *second* washing in order to pronounce the leprosy cleansed. Consequently, the second part of man's cleansing and the cleansing of a house from leprosy are both performed with *two birds and running water* (Lev. 14:4–7, 14:49–53).

One bird is killed for the other bird and the living bird is dipped in the blood and in the running water. As there are two washings, there are two parts to this ceremonial cleansing. Note the connection, Jesus died, dipped and washed us in His blood (Rev. 1:5). This is the first washing, the first cleansing, this is *justification*.

The second washing, the second cleansing is not done with blood but with running water. What does running water represent? A *flowing river*, therefore in John 7:38–39 it says:

> He that believeth on Me, as the scripture hath said, out of his belly shall *flow* rivers of living water (But this He spake of the Spirit, which they that believe on Him should

receive: for the Holy Ghost was not yet given; because that Jesus was not yet glorified.) (emphasis added).

Now notice this back in Leviticus 14:51, the bird to be killed was **over** the running water and the live bird was dipped in the running water. This tells of the work of the Holy Spirit being over us as a mantle till our self-life dies, and then His dwelling in us bringing true life. It was only after this second cleansing that the person, the garment or the house was pronounced clean. This second washing is *glorification in the Holy Spirit*. The living bird was then set free, justified and glorified. (See Romans 8:30.)

But there is one more point here. Before the second washing took place there was a *waiting period* of seven days. These seven days signify a period of grace, to wait for the "appearing or spreading of the leprosy." Upon the appearing or spreading it was unclean, and in the garment particularly as we know, it was burnt with fire. This is *sanctification*, as stated before. This waiting period is that period of grace after justification that gives us space to repent and remove our outward fleshly sins, moving away from the old life and into the new. As we move on, though, the normal experience for the believer is to see that even though the plague of sin has stopped spreading *outwardly* through wicked and selfish acts, there is the more *sinister plague inwardly* rooted in our very nature; an inherited sin that we must desperately want to be pronounced clean from.

Nevertheless, in our search to be free while in this waiting period, we find ourselves trapped and enslaved. This gives us the opportunity to see the necessity for something else, something more to take place. We will always be found "unclean" in this time of grace and need to pass through the Lord's baptism of fire; to be set free by His second cleansing, the living running water of God's Spirit. If you have never been brought to understand this need in your life, let's look at how deeply rooted sin is within us and gain more insight in the next chapter.

One final point before exploring this further, the leprous person who was cleansed went through the same ritual of having the blood put on the right ear, thumb and great toe (Lev. 14:14) as did Aaron and his sons, which was to consecrate them for the priesthood (Lev. 8:23). But for the person to be cleansed the ritual went one step more; the priest was to take a log of oil and place it *upon* the blood, meaning right over top of the blood of the right ear, thumb and toe the oil was to be placed; and the remaining oil was to be poured upon their head (Lev. 14:18–19)! Do you see? Once this issue of sin is dealt with in us, we *then* become consecrated as God's royal priesthood!

Chapter 6

DNA AND THE GENETIC FALL OF MAN

G OD'S FINGERPRINTS ARE in everything and through everything from us, to our planet we live on, to the universe (Romans 1:20). Job 38:4–5 tells us that the earth's foundations were the result of measurements and a stretched out line upon it. God is the great mathematician and has encoded His handiwork into everything that exists. This extends from the laws that govern the universe to the laws that govern our body. Whether scientists admit it themselves or not, science in itself is proving the wisdom behind the order and design and those law codes every day. Whether we realize it or not our entire lives are interacting with and using those law codes that make up the material world every moment of our lives. We are awake during the day and sleep at night. We plant crops in the spring, and harvest in the fall, according to the law of a plant's life cycle. Even the language of a race or nation is a code in itself to interpret the physical realm around us and communicate one to another. A code, according to the dictionary, is:

A systematized body of law (mathematics or Physics)

Any system of principles or regulations (the Torah or Mosaic Law code)

A set of signals, characters, or symbols used in communication (language)

A set of words, letters, or numerals, used for secrecy or brevity in transmitting messages[1]

God has encoded His secrets into every aspect of life, hiding each one of them as a piece in a puzzle, so when all the pieces of the mystery are discovered they become one *grand revelation* of Himself!

> Even the mystery which hath been hid from ages and from generations.
>
> —COLOSSIANS 1:26

> It is the glory of God to conceal a thing: but the honor of kings is to search out a matter.
>
> —PROVERBS 25:2

I think everyone enjoys a good mystery and enjoys even more finding out the ending. This is part of human nature that God has put within mankind; to explore and discover from child to adult. God is the master mystery writer not only on paper as in the encoding in the Torah (discovered by Israeli mathematician Eliyahu Rips), but in all the natural sciences and biological life itself. We as a created people engineer, create and construct things that exist on the earth, metal, wood, stone, clay, etc., but God is the *genetic engineer* creating the foundation of life through DNA. Let's focus on DNA a little bit and I believe we can draw out a mystery here that will help us unravel some Scripture, seeing more clearly what God's purpose is for His body.

Scientists have decoded the human genome, which is the collection of all your genes and DNA, since 1990. What is DNA? God wrote a chemical message or code consisting of about three billion chemical letters, which are the instructions for a human being.

The DNA molecule is in shape known as a double helix as shown below. Each horizontal line or step consists of two chemical letters: Cytosine and Guanine or Thymine and Adenine. They always come in those base pairs and go by their first letters C and G or T and A. Each step forms part of the code, which is the formula or program for a human body. The formation of genes and proteins that gives our three-dimensional characteristics start with the information and instructions received from the DNA.[2]

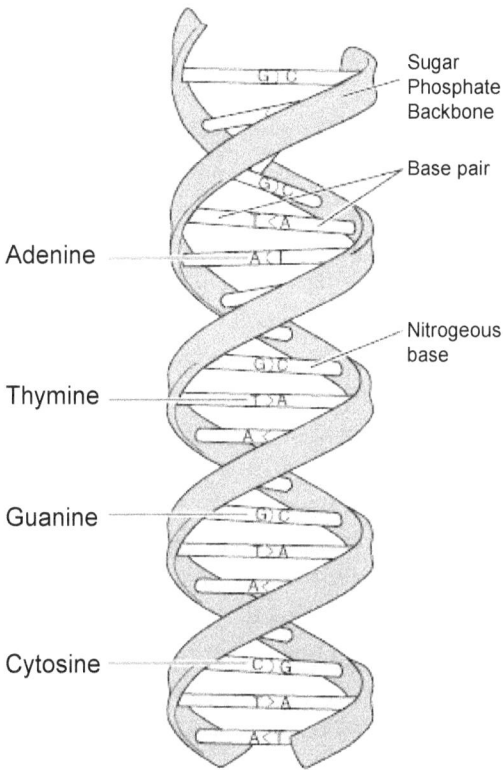

Scientists know that we all descend from a very small population and have about as much varying genetics now as we did from the beginning. Therefore we are 99.9 percent identical to everyone else, which is only one letter in a thousand different in our DNA between one another! Scientists have their own ideas about this founding population but to those who trust God's Word this beginning began with Adam and ran through his line to the time of the Flood, and from then we have all become descendants of Noah's family. This would confirm the observation of descending from a very small population. DNA is the *unbreakable thread* that traces every individual's life back to Adam. God wrote a chemical message for life on this planet and it has passed on from generation to generation ever since.

In the beginning God created the earth and everything in it including man in *His perfection*. God declares this perfection in Genesis 1:31; looking on what He had made He said it was "very good." So man was made in the perfection of God, and God's blessing was upon them. From this we can conclude that God wrote the chemical message of DNA for life perfect. We have to believe that, because God would not bless His creation and call it very good if it was not in the perfection of His image and likeness.

There was only one thing that man had to do to perpetuate and remain in God's perfection; it was to *obey* God by not eating from the tree of knowledge of good and evil. In Genesis 2:17 God makes it clear that man would *die* if he did eat of this tree. Therefore, a *potential* curse loomed in the background of all perfection.

God wrote in the DNA of man the heredity of Himself, therefore it would pass on to every generation. Ultimately God had fulfilled the desire of His heart by becoming the *Father* of a race of people. Furthermore, passing on the characteristics of God the Father would take no thought or effort because of the encoding of these instructions for every offspring in the future. Beautiful!

Man, though, chose a different course, exercising the liberty of his free will and disobeyed God's command. In a single moment of time their "eyes were opened" (Gen. 3:7) and their lives were immediately altered. What happened in that moment of time? *The genetic makeup of mankind was changed!* Man could no longer carry the heredity of God within himself because he could no longer be identified with God as his Father. Man had rebelled against God and through disobedience became sinful. Since there is no sin in God nor can be (James 1:13), man was no longer of His likeness and image, and by default became the bearer of the devil's likeness and image. The devil had succeeded in stealing the Fatherhood of God away from Him by deceit and became the father of the earthly race. Hence, Jesus told the Pharisees their father was the devil.

Man's perfect DNA code was *rewritten* to pass on the heredity of their new father, Satan. *Sin*, the *nature of sin* as well as *death* and every-thing related to it was *encoded into* man! Adam's perfect genetic code was now imperfect, it had become flawed and marred; it was cursed. It would now be those flawed and marred instructions that passed on to Adam's children through the generations to us. This must be the case, with the facts presented to us in the Bible and in science through logical deduction.

> As by one man sin entered into the world, and death by sin and so death *passed* upon *all* men for that *all* have sinned.
>
> Death reigned from Adam to Moses, *even over them that had not sinned after the similitude of Adam's transgression*, who is the figure of him that was to come.
>
> —ROMANS 5:12, 14

Even over them that had not sinned; like Adam, they inherited sin and death. How? Through man's DNA; it was written into him.

This is an excerpt from a dialogue between one of the scientists that worked on gathering all the letters of the DNA code for the U.S. government in the 80's and a reporter from the television presentation *NOVA*. Keep in mind that scientists who do not believe in creation always have their own timetable of when things took place, but their findings *always* validate truth rather than disprove it.[3]

> Eric Lander (scientist): The remarkable thing about our genome is how little gene is in it, we have three billion letters of DNA but only one to one and a half percent of it is gene.
>
> Robert Krulwich (Reporter): One and a half percent?
>
> S: The rest of it, 99 percent of it is stuff.
>
> R: Stuff, this is a technical term?
>
> S: More than half of your total DNA is not really yours, it consists of selfish DNA elements that some how got into

our genomes about a billion and a half years ago and have been hopping around making copies of themselves. To those selfish DNA elements we are merely a host for them.

R: Wait a minute we have in each and every one of our cells that carry DNA, we have these little, uh, their not beings, they are just hitchhiking hitchhikers?

S: Yeah, hitchhiking chunks of DNA.

R: They have been in us for how long?

S: About a billion and a half years or so.

R: And all they have done as far as you can say is stay there and multiple?

S: Well they move around.

R: And what is that? What do you call that? It's not an animal it's not a vegetable it's just...? [Author's note: the DNA found in us is similar to that found in every other living thing.]

S: It's just a gene that knows how to look out for itself and nothing else.

R: And it's just riding around in us through time?

S: Just riding around in us. The majority of our genome is this stuff not us.

R: Wow. It is a little humbling to think, that we the paragon of animals, the architects of great civilizations are used as taxi cabs by a bunch of free loading parasites that couldn't care less about us, but that's the mystery of it all.

To those who have knowledge of the living God "the mystery of it all" is being revealed. Here is a scientist who doesn't believe in God as Creator but with scientific observation has confirmed there are selfish DNA elements that are not us at all being passed from one person to another! A gene that cares nothing for us and only looks out for itself! Doesn't that have the same familiar ring as the corrupt nature of mankind? Have you ever observed the response between siblings just after watching a lovely, warm program about sharing? Time and again an argument will ensue over what is Sally's and Jimmy can't have it!

When people grow to be adults and put away these childish attitudes, they tend to think they are OK with God because they no longer commit outright selfish acts but "do good." The reality of this is that everything that was encoded into the child's DNA is still encoded into the adult, and there is nothing within themselves that can change this fact!

> We are all as an *unclean* thing, and *all* our righteousnesses
> are as filthy rags; and we *all* do fade as a leaf.
> — Isaiah 64:6, emphasis added

We know we are unclean by *scientific fact* and it is preposterous to think that some righteous acts on our part will change our state in the eyes of God.

Since man fell, God's heart never stopped longing to be the rightful Father of a people and He attempted to reclaim this position through the Mosaic Law code. In this way God was revealing a way of redemption, a way that sin could be charged, covered and removed; but it was also to act as a *mirror* for the interior man, to see our total depravity, and that even at our best sin and disobedience prevails. Now let's look at what Paul says in the seventh chapter of Romans:

> Wherefore the law is holy, and the commandment holy,
> and just, and good. Was then that which is good made
> death unto me? God forbid. But sin, that it might appear
> sin, working death in me by that which is good; that sin by
> the commandment might become exceeding sinful.
> —Romans 7:12–13

This is the reflection from the mirror of the law that men are to see within themselves. Then Paul states very clearly in verses 14–23 what is playing out through the heredity of mankind:

> v. 14"For we know that the law is spiritual: but I am carnal, sold under sin.

> v. 15 For that which I do I allow not: for what I would, that do I not; but what I hate that do I.

> v. 16 If then I do that which I would not, I consent onto the law that it is good.

> v. 17 Now then it is no more I that do it, but sin that dwelleth in me.

> v. 18 For I know that in me (that is, in my flesh,) dwelleth no good thing: for to will is present with me; but how to perform that which is good I find not.

> v. 19 For the good that I would I do not: but the evil which I would not, that I do.

> v. 20 Now if I do that I would not, it is no more I that do it, but sin that dwelleth in me.

> v. 21 I find then a law, that, when I would do good, evil is present with me.

> v. 22 For I delight in the law of God after the inward man:

> v. 23 But I see another law in my members, warring against the law of my mind, and bringing me into captivity to the law of sin which is in my members."

Let's summarize what Paul is saying: there is sin that dwells in him (v. 17); there is no "good thing" that dwells in his *flesh* (v. 18); it is no longer he who does evil but sin that dwells in him (v. 20). So then he says that he finds a law that no matter what, evil is there (v. 21); he delights in God's law but warring against the law of his mind (to do good) is a *law of sin*, which is *in his members* bringing him into *captivity*. Without the aid of a microscope, but by observation and revelation, Paul dictated these words approximately 2,000 years ago and declared that there were two laws: the law of God that stood for goodness, holiness and righteousness *outside* the man, and the law of sin that governs evil *inside* him.

The law that governs evil within us is intertwined in the same genetic code that governs the color of our hair or the height of our stature. Jesus said:

> Neither shalt thou swear by thy head, because thou canst not make one hair white or black.
>
> —MATTHEW 5:36

Again:

> Which of you by taking thought can add one cubit unto his stature?
>
> —MATTHEW 6:27

Jesus used these as examples because it is not within the power of man to change the genetic code that governs these things. Paul and Jesus are declaring the same thing: just as people cannot concentrate hard enough to make themselves taller or change the color of their hair, nor can they concentrate hard enough to make sin disappear. These things are written into the formula of man; it is *who you are*, buried deep within your *members*, deep within your *flesh*. How deep? Scientifically we know that the DNA, the instruction book for every individual lies within the nucleus of every cell of the entire body! Now we can understand the Lord's command:

> If any man's seed of copulation [male sperm] go out from him, then he shall wash all his flesh in water, and be unclean

until the even. And every garment, and every skin [here is the same connection again discovered in the previous chapter], whereon is the seed of copulation, shall be washed with water, and be unclean until the even. The women also with whom man shall lie with seed of copulation, they shall both bathe themselves in water, and be unclean until the even.

—LEVITICUS 15:16–18, EMPHASIS ADDED

God can see right into man's DNA and see the specks and flaws that make up the corrupt nature of mankind. Therefore, when that tainted genetic code went forth in the man's sperm it was unclean. By this God was revealing to us once again that the problem with man lies within his genetic makeup at the *cellular level*; and as a ceremonial cleansing the man and the woman were to wash all their flesh in water. (This should not be confused with Hebrews 13:4 by the bed being undefiled. The bed here was undefiled *morally*, but in Leviticus it is a genetic issue that the scripture is dealing with.)

Let's look into the Scriptures to find some correlation between our genetics and the language used to describe it.

And the LORD spake unto Moses, saying, Speak unto Aaron, saying, Whosoever he be of thy seed in their generations that hath any blemish, let him not approach to offer the bread of his God. For whatsoever man he be that hath a blemish, he shall not approach: a blind man, or a lame, or he that hath a flat nose, or any thing superfluous, or a man that is brokenfooted, or brokenhanded, or crookback[ed], or a dwarf, or that hath a blemish in his eye, or be scurvy, or scabbed, or hath his stones broken; no man that hath a blemish of the seed of Aaron the priest shall come nigh to offer the offerings of the LORD made by fire: he hath a blemish; he shall not come nigh to offer the bread of his God. He shall eat the bread of his God, both of the most holy, and of the holy. Only he shall not go in unto the vail, nor come nigh unto to the altar, because he hath a blemish; that he profane not my sanctuaries: for I the LORD do sanctify them.

—LEVITICUS 21:16–23, EMPHASIS ADDED

God uses the term "blemish" very heavily here to describe all of these imperfections; even a flat nose, or a dwarf, or anything superfluous (that which is obviously out of proportion), which come out of the genetic formation of the person. Those without understanding can blame God here for being cruel to separate such people when they cannot even help how they turn out, especially in our day when all handicaps are embraced! But God is drawing us a much bigger picture than what is at face value. He is telling us that we are all genetically tainted on the inside, and that it requires no blemish to approach Him. God said they may still partake and eat His *bread*, but to *approach* His presence they could not.

In Scripture God continues to use the term blemish when referring to animals. They had to be *genetically perfect* when offered as a sacrifice. In Numbers 29:17 and 26 the word "spot" is also used *interchangeably* to refer to the same thing as we see in Numbers 29:2. With this established in our minds we could ask the question, why are scientists interested in mapping out the DNA code? They are in fact looking for all the *spots* and *blemishes* in our DNA! Because the blemish of the law of sin was encoded into us, that curse has flowed throughout our DNA, which has brought sickness and disease. Scientists know that the keys to understanding sickness and disease and to finding potential cures are wrapped up in our DNA. The mapping of all the chemical letters has given them *the model of what perfect DNA would look like*, maybe not looking at it as a complete whole, but little sections of it at a time. They discovered that one single letter out of our chemical base pairs *can cause disease*; the reporter from before described this as "one insignificant dot buried in our DNA." Just one letter missing, one spot out of order and we are marred with disease or at the least carriers of an imperfect or defective genetic code that is passed on to the next generation. We carry uncleanness within ourselves genetically and *no one is immune.* The Bible impresses that upon us quite clearly. We are *all* as an unclean thing (Isa. 64:6).

> All have sinned and fall short.
> —ROMANS 3:23, NKJV

> Death passed upon all men for that *all* have sinned.
> —ROMANS 5:12, EMPHASIS ADDED

Consider this in Deuteronomy 32:4–5:

> He [God] is the Rock (emphasis added).

First, why is God described as a Rock? Because rocks don't change, they are the same yesterday, today and forever. It is man that lost his identity with the Rock and is changed through man's genetic fall. Then amazingly the verse goes on to state:

> His work is perfect: for all His ways are judgment: a God of truth and without iniquity, just and right is He. They have corrupted themselves, their *spot* is not the *spot* of *His children*: they are a perverse and crooked generation (emphasis added).

I believe with all my heart that it's no accident that the terminology used to describe the corruption and depravity of man coincides with defective spots on our DNA being discovered in modern science.

Let's look a little closer. Scientists have discovered that two or three chemical letters in a row can be missing out of the 3 billion. This causes a faulty gene, and because the genes make up the proteins in our bodies, (which takes us from the one-dimensional map of DNA to a three-dimensional human), that causes a disfigured or deformed protein, and disease is the result. For example, this is what a normal gene looks like:[4]

TCTGTAGAGAGTAGCAGT

The error that a scientist discovered that can cause breast cancer looks like this:

TCTGTAGAG[ ][ ] TAGCAGT

Two letters are missing, so the normal DNA code gets scrunched together. If I take a piece of cloth and lay it flat on a table, then I pinch a little section of it together, what have I created? It is no longer flat as it should be, but has a *wrinkle* in it! Are you getting the picture? We are spotted and wrinkled *genetically*! In the King James Version there are only two references to the word *wrinkle*.

> And thou hast filled me with wrinkles, which is a witness against me: and my leanness rising up in me beareth witness to my face.
>
> —JOB 16:8

Job describes his sore sickness using the term *wrinkles*. In Job's case wrinkles *equaled* sickness. We know that Job was smitten with sore boils from the sole of his foot unto his crown (Job 2:7). Isaiah, therefore, uses Job's description symbolically to describe Israel's "sickly" condition:

> From the sole of the foot even unto the head there is no soundness in it.
>
> —ISAIAH 1:6

In like manner this description of sickness is for our sake. So let's glean from Job's experience to make some connections. If Job's condition, described in Job 2:7 was used for Israel in Isaiah 1:6, *what* was it describing?

> A people laden with iniquity, a seed of evildoers, children that are corrupters.
>
> —ISAIAH 1:4

Remember how God pronounced the seed of copulation unclean in Leviticus, and again the people that had corrupted themselves were not the spot of His children in Deuteronomy 32:5? These references can be linked back to Job that we may perceive a new level of insight, which goes down into the depth of man. So where was Job afflicted? (See Job 2:4–5.) Satan tempts God to put forth His hand and touch his bone and his flesh. Why? Look at the other references in scripture that talk about flesh and bone starting in Genesis 2:21–23.

God took one of Adam's ribs for the purpose that woman would be genetically identical to the original formula, and Adam declares this is "now bone of my bones, and flesh of my flesh." It was the way of saying we are *one and the same* genetically. Laban said to Jacob:

> Surely thou art my bone and my flesh.
>
> —Genesis 29:14

Again:

> I am your bone and your flesh.
>
> —Judges 9:2

And again:

> Then came all the tribes of Israel to David unto Hebron, and spake, saying, Behold, we are thy bone and thy flesh.
>
> —2 Samuel 5:1

In each verse the meaning is that they are the same *kinship*, the same *genetic makeup*, they are *family* with the same forefathers. So in other words, what Satan was really asking God to do was to touch the genetic makeup of Job, touch his innermost being where it all works! Job described his affliction as "wrinkles"; and now we know scientifically that these wrinkles in our inner most being, deep in our DNA cause disease!

From this knowledge we can unfold God's heart and begin to see His ultimate purpose for us through Christ. As long as man is in a genetically sinful state he is blemished. It is genetically unjust for God to take possession of us on the inside in a flawed state; God cannot dwell with the law of sin in man and man cannot carry the heredity of God, just as darkness cannot be light. So what is God's heart and plan? He desires to genetically make right that which was stolen from man at the Fall and bring us into the lineage of Christ.

> Behold, the days come, saith the Lord, that I will make a new covenant with the house of Israel, and with the house of Judah: not according to the covenant that I made with their fathers in the day that I took them by the hand to bring them out of the land of Egypt; which my covenant they brake, although I was an husband unto them, saith the LORD.
>
> —JEREMIAH 31:31–32

Remember that this covenant was to prove the total depravity within man. Now let's see what this new covenant is that God desires to make.

> I will put my law in their inward parts, and write it in their hearts; and will be their God, and they shall be my people.
>
> —JEREMIAH 31:33

Do you understand what this means? I will put *my* law in their *inward parts* and *write it* in their hearts! Do you think that God is going to take those stone tablets that have His commandments written on them and stuff them into us? No! He wants to rewrite the genetic inheritance of Himself back into our "inward parts" deep down in our DNA! Through the new covenant God wants to encode His life back into us that Adam and Eve lost; the code of *original life*; the code that made up "God" in man's DNA. That is what was to be inherited through all generations with no knowledge of sin, sickness and death! Did you think that God was going to put his rules and regulations that are the strength of sin into you?

The sting of death is sin; and the strength of sin is the law.

—1 CORINTHIANS 15:56

No, God wants to take us back to the "very good" when He created man perfect. One may argue that this refers to our spirit man. If this were the case I believe the Lord would *not* have used the choice words *inward parts*, but used the term *inner man* as Paul does. Nor would God refer to His law that needs to be put there. It is not the spirit of man that holds the problem. Jesus said, "the spirit is willing, but the flesh is weak." It is the flesh of man that holds within it the law of sin that wars against God, not the spirit. It is that law of sin that needs to be changed.

Even in our finite wisdom we can comprehend that we need to reverse a problem where it is defective and not try and fix it by strengthening something else in the system that doesn't need it. If you applied that kind of thinking to the world around us nothing would function as it should and many breakdowns would occur. Therefore, to solve a problem in the physical world you must replace the weakened part. If we would take this approach, why wouldn't God? Jesus confirms the heart of God in this saying:

Neither do men put new wine into old bottles; else the bottles break, and the wine runneth out, and the bottles perish: but they put new wine into new bottles, and both are preserved.

—MATTHEW 9:17

Furthermore, when God says in Jeremiah 31:33 that He "will be their God and they shall be My people" (emphasis added), He is reinstating His Fatherhood with a people that bear within themselves, once again, His likeness and image genetically. As we established before, Adam and Eve lost God's heredity to bear His likeness and image through the genetic fall. If that never happened, then we know that their children would have known God by heredity, without being taught by external law. This is why Jeremiah goes on to say:

> And they shall teach no more every man his neighbour, and every man his brother, saying, Know the LORD: for they shall all know me, from the least of them unto the greatest of them, saith the LORD: for I will forgive their iniquity, and I will remember their sin no more.
>
> —JEREMIAH 31:34

Have you every stopped to think of certain gestures that you do, or the way you write your *P's* and *Q's*, that they are the same as your mother's or father's? This is because you carry the memory of them and these things through your genetic code. Therefore, God is saying that each person would carry the memory of Himself and His nature within every cell of our physical being! And God finally says He will forgive their iniquity and remember their sin no more. Why? Because He will be looking upon His own law within man and no longer the law of sin. Amen.

So how was God going to perform this? You guessed it; He needed Adam Number Two, Jesus Christ. Let's draw reference now to the Lord's life starting in the Old Testament. In Exodus 12:5 the Lord commands Moses that the Passover lamb is to be without blemish. We know that the Lord is our Passover Lamb and that He was without blemish.

> …the precious blood of Christ, as of a lamb without blemish and without spot.
>
> —1 PETER 1:19

God has wanted to have a people as in the beginning, but He needed to condemn the disobedience of Adam and the law of sin in his members, in his flesh, and appease His justice. He needed to begin afresh with a new race from their original genetic state. We know that Jesus succeeded in paying the penalty for sin and became the first son (as Paul states that Jesus is the first born among many brethren) under the new covenant. But how? God needed another *genetically perfect human*; this is exactly why Paul calls Jesus the last Adam, the second man (1 Cor. 15:47). As Adam was created genetically perfect without any spot, wrinkle or blemish in him, so was Christ; and what Jesus was on earth is exactly what Adam was in the beginning.

The original formula for man was *written* into Christ as it was from the beginning. This is why Jesus called God, His Father and also said, "He that hath seen Me hath seen the Father" (John 14:9), because in His genetic makeup there was no flaw, no defect, nothing marred or tainted, and nothing out of order. God could look right into Jesus's inward parts and see nothing that wasn't Himself! Therefore, Christ for *our example* could receive all of God and God could receive all of Christ.

> For it pleased the Father that in Him should all fulness dwell.
> —COLOSSIANS 1:19

> For in Him dwelleth all the fulness of the Godhead bodily.
> —COLOSSIANS 2:9

Jesus sacrificially made Himself of no reputation (Phil. 2:6–7) to become our model in His humanity. How was this accomplished?

> Now the birth of Jesus Christ was on this wise: when as his mother Mary was espoused to Joseph, before they came together, she was found with child of the Holy Ghost.
> —MATTHEW 1:18

Because Mary was a virgin and before the genetic uncleanness passed to her from the *seed of fallen man*, Jesus Christ was formed of God from the *"dust of woman"* in her womb, just as Adam was formed by God in the beginning from the *womb of the earth*. Jesus declared:

> For the prince of this world [the devil] cometh, and hath nothing in Me.
> —JOHN 14:30, EMPHASIS ADDED

This "nothing" that Jesus speaks of has to be referring to the *totality* of His makeup. But for Jesus Christ to become the *first* child *reestablishing* God's *Fatherhood* and begin a new race, a new family of people, He would have to pass the *test of temptation* where Adam failed. But with one important difference: Adam didn't have the Holy Ghost! The Holy Ghost was the completion of Christ and the completion of man; which Adam lacked. If Adam and Eve had eaten from the tree of life *first* and received the completing work of the Holy Ghost within them, they wouldn't have failed where Christ succeeded.

Nevertheless, because of Jesus's triumph, again I repeat, He became the first among many brethren, that we may be conformed to the image of the Son (Rom. 8:29). The Father desires a people that are in every aspect according to His original plan, which we see revealed in Christ. Jesus *didn't* address people's diseases or sickness. He said, "Be clean" or "Be made whole," this is the Father's heart. I believe that we have become closed in our thinking towards the *perfection* and *completeness* that God established in the life of Christ that is meant for us because again we misunderstand what that would mean. Job states a *fact* that we need to give our attention to when he described his sickness:

> Thou hast filled me with wrinkles, which is *a witness against me: and my leanness rising up in me beareth witness to my face.*
>
> —JOB 16:8, EMPHASIS ADDED

The Lord's body is filled with sickness and disease, and death overtakes many; this is not a representation of the life of Christ or the Father's heart. This no doubt is a witness against us, staring us in the face, showing us that we are not walking in God's new covenant. I want this firmly established in your mind: if we go back before man's DNA fell into corruption and inherited sin, Adam and Eve would have borne children identical to the genetic makeup found in Jesus Christ! They would have borne children with God's genetic characteristics, right down to you and me in this generation; that was God's original intention! You would've been born from birth with *all* the characteristics that were found in Christ, with *all* His potential. You would still look like you, but God the Father would have been as natural to you as your natural parents are now, and your ancestors before you. But instead the unbreakable DNA link from Adam brought to each family is genetically sinful. God wants us back to what we were naturally supposed to be in the first place. Let's continue to draw out this picture from Scripture:

> Whereby are given unto us exceeding great and precious promises: that by these ye might be partakers of the divine nature, having escaped the corruption that is in the world through lust.
>
> —2 PETER 1:4

Peter talks about being partakers of the divine nature. We can *legally* conclude that this divine nature was the nature of Christ, which would be the *original nature* given to Adam before the Fall. This was to be our nature, and can be through Christ, but how? The same way it would be there in the first place, it would be put in our inward parts, no different than the nature that comes out of you from your earthly parents. So God wants to put *the law of His nature in your inward parts*, re-write it into you! Do you have to think about acting like your parents in different aspects of your life? No, it is who you have become because you inherited their genes. The same is true with God's desire. If God's nature is put in your genes, will you have to think about being like God? No! You will have become His likeness. We need to understand this depth. This and only this is what eliminates the law of sin and God's external law that strengthens the law of sin in our lives. Did Jesus come only to save our soul or our spirit? Or did He come to save the whole man? Be made whole! "Be Holy for I am Holy," (Lev. 11:44) spirit, soul and body. This is why the Bible tells of a birth! A birth into what? A birth into God's perfect and complete divine order in the whole man!

> He that committeth sin is of the devil; for the devil sinneth from the beginning. For this purpose the Son of God was

manifested, that He might destroy the works of the devil. Whosoever is born of God doth not commit sin; for his *seed* remaineth in him: and he cannot sin, because He is *born of God*.

—1 John 3:8–9, emphasis added

Where is Jesus going to destroy the works of the devil in you? Where the law of sin was birthed; in your members, in your inward parts, in your genetic makeup. He's not going to change your eyes or ears, nor your stature, but those parts that are not you and those spots and blemishes that come from the curse. Is anything too hard for our God? Is His hand waxed short? You are to be "born" (not only your spirit) of God, and John uses the choice word seed to bring forth this understanding. The "seed" as learned previously from the "seed of copulation" carries within it all genetic information for the offspring; therefore, this being the beginning where the code of life is passed on, (man's tainted seed being unclean), God's seed rewrites His nature into us and we cannot sin! Why? John said it, "Because he is born of God" (emphasis added). You are no longer identified with sin or anything to do with sin. It is no longer a part of you! This is what brings glory to our God. It is God's heart that He presents a family to Himself, *identical* to His Son:

> Not having *spot*, or *wrinkle*, or any such thing; but that it should be *holy* and without *blemish*."
>
> —Ephesians 5:27, emphasis added

How has God intended to accomplish this? He can't do it by natural procreation, which is tainted, as we know. So how? The same way Jesus Christ was conceived: by the Holy Spirit. Now if at this point I have brought you to a climax and let you down because I have said "by the Holy Spirit," and you yawn and say "been there, done that," Then you need go from one corner of your mind to the other and gather up all the "little" Holy Spirit knowledge and experience you have and throw it out the window as fast as you can. Then open your ears to what the Spirit sayeth unto the church. It has been people's carnal minds that have brought the Holy Spirit down to the size of a pea! There is a realm and a depth in the Holy Spirit that you haven't even gotten hold of, and when you do, it will expand and widen and you will never conceive of an end!

So it is by the Holy Spirit that God did and would birth this new race, beginning with Christ. I want to bring out a little more evidence to our kinship and identity with Christ to further conclude God's desire. When Jesus rose from the dead we read:

> Handle Me and see; for a spirit hath not flesh and bones, as ye see Me have.
>
> —LUKE 24:39

The Lord uses the same description, "flesh and bones" as we discovered before. He took back the body that was given to Him by God and was establishing that a new race of people had begun, who would be identified with Himself in every way, and declares:

> I ascend unto My Father and your Father and to My God, and your God.
>
> —JOHN 20:17

The original order, the original kinship with God was reestablished, and Paul states this fact:

> For we are members of His body, of *His flesh*, and of *His bones*.
>
> —EPHESIANS 5:30, EMPHASIS ADDED

Paul understood this terminology from the Old Testament and would have used it as an expression for family in his times. Again we read:

> He is the head of the Body, the church: who is the beginning.
>
> —COLOSSIANS 1:18

Let me ask you. Is your body genetically different from your head? No. The DNA that is buried in the cells of your head is the same that is buried in your body; they are identical!

> As He is, so are we in this world.
> —1 JOHN 4:17

Through Christ, God wants to rewrite and put His inherited nature into you by the Holy Ghost.

> Forasmuch as ye are manifestly declared to be the epistle of Christ ministered by us, *written not with ink*, but with the Spirit of the living God; not in tables of stone, but *in fleshly tables of the heart.*
> —2 CORINTHIANS 3:3, EMPHASIS ADDED

God wants to make man altogether perfect as in the beginning, being altogether like Himself, but we have lost the *purpose of God* in our minds, leaving us no direction. It was disobedience that brought the blemished sin upon man; let us not be disobedient to the heavenly vision and neglect the totality of this salvation!

If God can change Moses's hand leprous one moment and turn it back the next, He can remove every spot and wrinkle out of your life in a moment of time. The fall of man's nature and his genetic identity with God changed in a single moment, and in a single moment the promise of God's Spirit was poured out in Acts 2 reversing the curse of that genetic fall! A family was born of His seed and His Spirit that inherited the very characteristics and nature of God!

Chapter 7

THE FULLNESS OF GOD IN MAN

Grace and peace be multiplied unto you through the knowledge of God, and of Jesus our Lord, according as His divine power hath given unto us *all things* that pertain unto *life and godliness*, through the knowledge of Him that hath called us to glory and virtue.

—2 PETER 1:2–3, EMPHASIS ADDED

Whom He did predestinate, them He also called: and whom He called, them He also justified: and whom He justified, them He also *glorified*. What shall we say then to these things? If God be for us, who can be against us? He that spared not His own Son, but delivered Him up for us all, how shall He not with Him also *freely give us all things*?

—ROMANS 8:30–32, EMPHASIS ADDED

WITH PAUL'S QUESTIONS, I ask a similar one. If we are destined to be the Bride of Christ, why is it such a hard thing in our minds to conceive that God desires man to be full of Himself? God's desire from the Creation was to give man the opportunity to receive the essence of His fullness. The word essence in Webster's dictionary means the fundamental nature and quality; a substance distilled or extracted from another substance and having the special qualities of the original substance; perfume.[1]

Please understand that it does *not* mean that we become omnipotent, omniscient, or omnipresent in that regard, but He can show us the things to come and teach all things from His perspective. And we become that quality of God and share in His fullness as Christ did. The word *perfume* is a wonderful description of this.

God sent Christ into the earth to be the example of His desire, that with Christ we could share in the Father's life and presence. God created man in His likeness and image. We know from the previous chapter that man was created in God's perfection, and had the capacity to become the incarnate of God through His Spirit and be complete in all things. The Holy Spirit inhabiting the sinless flesh of man was to be His completion plan that would make him *not only a son by genetic perfection,* but (by partaking of the "tree of life" that was there from the beginning) a son through God's endless life, His living water. He would be God-like and carry about God's attributes. Man would carry the substance and presence of God, from God's mind and His emotions to His power and glory, and He still desires to share with His people today. This was to be God's marriage to man, the *closest union* possible. God's Spirit would possess man and man's spirit would possess God, and both would inhabit together under "one roof" in the body of man. God would forever be present with man and man would be forever present with God. God uses the symbolism in natural marriage to reveal this:

> And *they* shall be *one* flesh.
>
> —GENESIS 2:24, EMPHASIS ADDED

And again,

> Male and female created He them; and blessed them, and called *their name Adam.*
>
> —GENESIS 5:2, EMPHASIS ADDED

In God's eyes they were "one" and inseparable. That is why divorce in marriage was never God's mind, because it is a representation of His own plan of union with man.

God would have completed the oneness with man that He desired and fulfilled the longing within man for the same. But, it was this *longing* in man that the devil used to steal God's bride away from Him through subtlety, and inhabit man's body for himself; with fear and self-consciousness as the first results. Man was created a *neutral* being *meant* to be inhabited, but given a free will, man had to *choose* to eat from the tree of life and welcome this divine union between himself and God. If man had done so the presence of God with him would have taken him *safely* through any waters of temptation. Remember that the deed of disobedience was done when God's presence wasn't with Adam and Eve at the time.

Jesus Christ, in His humanity came to exemplify this divine union between God in man and man in God as it was in God's heart from the beginning. Jesus has transported us back, before the Fall, before sinful flesh to see what the first *completed human being* would look like! God created man to have dominion in all things, both in earth and in the Spirit as declared:

> Replenish the earth and subdue it: and have dominion over
> the fish of the sea, and over the fowl of the air, and every
> living thing that moveth upon the earth.
> —GENESIS 1:28

> It is your Father's good pleasure to give you the Kingdom.
> —LUKE 12:32

God created Adam from the dust of the earth. He was therefore God's son through the perfection of His creation. Therefore, man, being children of God's creation, were given the right of inheritance over the earth and have dominion in it. This is no different then you inheriting the possessions of your earthly father. So, man was a son of God, but only by creation. He needed to become a son of God's *substance* and *being* before he could inherit all things: namely God's kingdom, and the things of His Spirit. Man had to accept the divine proposal of God to become one being, one "flesh" in the inner man, in the spirit of man with God. That man's soul, his mind, will, and emotions would melt into the living Spirit of God; and God's mind, will, and emotions would melt into man's soul. The two would be fused together and become "Adam," *one identity in desire and purpose.* The devil knew God's purpose and coveted this special affection given to man. Therefore, he deceived Eve by telling her she would become "like" God "another way." Adam needed to accept this union between

God and himself to be declared the son of God by the uncreated life of God's spirit possessing him. This was to give him the right of inheritance by Sonship over God's kingdom and have dominion in it too. Adam would have become the rightful heir to the throne, ruling and reigning with the Triune Godhead, Father, Son and Holy Spirit.

Jesus Christ reveals this from His life in the days of His flesh. Paul says in Philippians 2:7–8

> But made Himself [Jesus] of no reputation, and took upon Him the form of a servant, and was *made in the likeness of men*: and being found in fashion as a man, he humbled Himself... (emphasis added).

Jesus came in created flesh to reinstate a part of humanity that was lost. It was almost as if history were replaying itself, but better, with the intended results. Therefore, following the original order, Jesus gave up His Father's throne for a time and became the Son of God by creation first, as Adam was, created *genetically perfect* as in the beginning. Therefore Christ became the rightful heir over the earth, to have dominion in it. But He was not declared the rightful heir to God's kingdom until He accepted the union between the Holy Spirit and Himself; exactly as it was offered to Adam through the tree of life. Matthew, Mark and Luke's Gospels all agree that first, the Holy Spirit descended upon Jesus and took possession of Him; and then the Lord spoke from heaven:

> Thou art my beloved Son; in thee I am well pleased.
> —LUKE 3:22

This was the declaration of the Sonship of Christ, the rightful heir to the throne in Spirit and Life. Jesus, fulfilling all righteousness and laying out the rightful order of redemption, stepped back into Adam's "sandals." He became the first man to be "*born again*" according to the Father's original intention for man laid out from the foundation of the world.

Born, not of blood, nor of the will of the flesh, nor of the will of man, but of God.

—JOHN 1:13

This gives us a deeper understanding of what Jesus was referring to when He told Nicodemus that:

Except a man be born again, he cannot see the kingdom of God.

—JOHN 3:3

Consider this: the disciples received revelation from God; Peter declared Jesus to be the Christ and Jesus told him God revealed it to him. They even did "works" for the kingdom, including Judas Iscariot, but are these things what made them born again of God after the original plan for man? No! When did they become born of God? When they received the Holy Spirit in like manner as Christ did, when they were baptized with the baptism that He was baptized with. It was then that He gave them power to become (or be declared) Sons of God (John 1:12).

It was only then that the keys of the kingdom could be granted, and inherited dominion be given to the disciples in *all things*. It had to be through the right of Sonship as from the beginning of creation. And they were affirmed to be Sons by power and authority working through them, as was the Lord. They were made one; as the Father was in Jesus and Jesus was in the Father, they were made one in them. The glory which God gave Jesus, Jesus gave to them that, they would be one with the Godhead; Jesus in them and the Father in Jesus that they would be perfected in oneness. (See John 17:21–23, author's paraphrase.)

Jesus was not praying that they would be one in the community of humanity together; no this was a spiritual uniting of God to every person individually who would accept this truth. Jesus is the truth and this was His personal understanding; therefore, He was praying that the Father's desire would once more have the opportunity to be fulfilled. This has been the Father's desire from the beginning and this has been the sum of Christ's redemption. The Holy Spirit given to man as it was meant to be in the Garden of Eden is the crowning victory of Jesus's life, death, resurrection and ascension.

After the early church, we have been failing in our generations to comprehend the power behind the Holy Spirit given to man, and this divine union laid out for him from the foundation of the world. Imagine yourself as Adam before the Fall after eating from the tree of life. Receiving this oneness through the Holy Spirit and enveloped by His love, power, glory, life and all that God is, your potential would be incalculable. This is the restoration of man through Christ's victory; this is Christ's "full salvation."

God's plan for man is not a religion, but a state of being; a life-form conceived of God, knowing Him in Spirit and in Truth. The Holy Spirit is the key that separates religion from reality and life!

Accepting what Jesus did on the cross is not the only part of living the Christian life. In fact this is not life at all; we are merely justified. There is absolutely no "LIFE" in justification, but it is an act of pardoning. Our text at the beginning states that those He justified He also glorified. How does this pertain to us? In every way; this is our destiny, to be fully as the Father was to Jesus through Sonship in the Spirit. Don't be deceived, this is not a process, this is an instantaneous life-changing event. As it was on the day of Pentecost, God came as a rushing mighty wind. If we think of the Holy Spirit coming into man as a process, He would be at best an influence and not a person. This is clearly unscriptural. Man was created with the capacity to hold all of God as we see through Jesus's life. Just as a man has the capacity to hold within himself a legion of demons (3,000–6,000) and be possessed by them, the contrary is true when the Holy Spirit takes possession of us. Therefore, we become all that God is, in will, in life, in nature, and in mind; just as the demon possessed becomes the personification of the demon's will, life, nature and mind. As Paul states:

Nevertheless I live; yet not I, but Christ liveth in me.

—GALATIANS 2:20

You may question, how this can be? You are not Jesus and were not born sinless. As we have discussed in the previous chapters, the Lord's sacrifice and victory has made provision for you to be at equal standing with Him as He was in His humanity. The very life that Jesus lived out in His flesh, His oneness with the Father, is offered to us. The position before Adam's transgression is where we can begin through Christ. He justified you and covered your sins so you could seek the Lord and become yielded to Him and He could hear you. Then He sends down His baptism of fire from off His altar and consumes everything that defiles the house, and rewrites His law in your inward parts. Now the Holy Spirit takes possession of a new, clean vessel and makes His abode within you, and His continual abiding presence, power and life remains forever.

Listen to Maria Woodworth-Etter's account. The power of the Holy Spirit came down as a cloud. It was brighter than the sun. She was covered and wrapped up in it. Her body was as light as the air. It seemed that heaven had come down. She was baptized with the Holy Spirit, and fire and power, which never left her. There was liquid fire and the angels were all around her in the fire and the glory. This was her testimony.[2]

Dear people of God, we have made God's hand short and our eyes have become dim to the depths of salvation Christ has attained for us. Just as no one goes down into water baptism the same, no two people have to experience the Holy Spirit taking possession of them in the same way. As we discussed previously, tongues were specifically for the establishment of the early church. You need to understand I am not attempting to remove tongues out of the baptism experience. They are still available for God to do as He wills with each individual, but we are stumbling over a pebble.

If we consider the testimonies of the spiritual giants of the faith, whether they spoke in tongues or not and wrote about it or not, they did not make this their cornerstone. Their cornerstone was God Himself, which gave them the power and authority working through their lives! Maria Woodworth-Etter didn't have claims of speaking in tongues, but look at what she does testify to. John G. Lake sought God's sanctification as a separate experience first, but when the Holy Spirit came, it was currents of electrifying power and a tenderness of love, *God's very nature* that he testifies to, and is predominate throughout his writings thereafter. John Lake does testify to speaking in tongues, but declares that he was unable to speak English, which again reinforces what we learned before that God comes to prove to the individual that their will is now in submission to His. Rees Howells says he was transported into another realm, within the sacred veil, where the Father, the Savior and the Holy Ghost live; there he heard God speaking to him. Rees also speaks of the banner of love over him and the floods of joy. Smith Wigglesworth declares that the fire fell: "It seems as though God bathed me in power" he was filled with the joy of the consciousness of Jesus's cleansing blood. Smith also declares he could not reproduce the tongues he spoke, but received the gift of tongues to use at will nine months later. Do you see He was under divine control just like John Lake? D.L. Moody testifies to power and joy, filling to such an extent that he had to ask God to withhold His hand, lest he die on the spot from joy. Charles Finney testifies of feeling the impression, like a wave of electricity, going through him, body and soul. It seemed to come in waves of liquid love. It did not seem like water, but rather the breath of God that seemed to fan him like immense wings that literally moved his hair like a passing breeze. He says that no words can describe the wonderful love that was shed abroad in his heart. He too like Moody cried out that he should die if these waves continued, and told the Lord he couldn't bear it any more. He uses the same words that Paul writes:

> The love of God is shed abroad in our hearts by the Holy Ghost which is given unto us.
>
> —ROMANS 5:5

Notice everyone encountered God's eternal Spirit in a *different* way, but I want you to look at a couple of writings and *consider the commonality* that became the focus afterward:

God wants you to be so immersed and covered and flooded with the light and revelation of the Holy Spirit, the third person of the Trinity, that your whole body will be filled, and not only filled but also covered over until you walk in the presence of the power of God. This is an interpretation of tongues: God's life for your life, His light for your darkness, His revelation for your closed brain. He brings forth new order in divine power until you will be changed into another man, until your very nature will be burning with a burning within you of divine purifying until you are like one who has come from the presence of the Glory to exhibit truths that God has revealed to you. In your lot, in your day, the power of another covering, girding you with the power of truth.[3]

—Smith Wigglesworth

When the Holy Spirit gets possession of a person, he is a new man entirely. His whole being becomes saturated with divine power. We become a habitation of Him who is all light, all revelation, all power, and all love. Yes, God the Holy Spirit is manifested within us in such a way that it is glorious.[4]

—Smith Wigglesworth

Jesus went to heaven in order that the very treasury of the heart of the eternal God might be unlocked for your benefit and that out of the very soul of the eternal God, the streams of His life and nature would possess you from the crown of your head to the sole of your feet and that there would be just as much of the eternal God in your toenails and in your brain as each is capable of containing. In other words, from the very soles of your feet to the last hair on the top of your head, every cell of your being would be residence of the Spirit of the living God. Man is made alive by God, and with God, by the Spirit. And in the truest sense, man is the dwelling place of God, the house of God, the tabernacle of the Most High.[5]

—JOHN G. LAKE

The Spirit produces a new walk, a new speech, a new manner of life. There will be power in that life. That life will be dominated and controlled by the Holy Spirit.[6]

—KATHRYN KUHLMAN

Think about it, would this not be God's real intent for every individual? Of course, He is no respecter of persons. Let's get to the real issue and stop excusing why we are not living and walking in this God-filled life and power. When the Holy Spirit comes He will glorify you; He will take that which is Christ's and give it to you, that you may bear fruit and glorify Christ. Every demon that has inhabited you through the door of your flesh, and every spot of darkness, He drives out with His presence and light. He does this that the whole house will be filled with light and glory with no darkness in it!

We are called to be children of the living God who demonstrate His life and power in miracles, signs and wonders, to the world. If we were giving the world the real thing, every church building would be packed out, because a city on a hill cannot be hid. Let's stop feeding on the crumbs of Christianity pretending we're full; living out a form of godliness, denying the power we lack. We must see our desolation and become desperate for more. We must tarry at Jerusalem till we are equipped and qualified with His power and life, that the world and His church may know "there is a God in Israel," that the Christ is alive and has come to inhabit His people!

Jesus Christ thought it not robbery to be equal with God, but left the bosom of the Father and through the Holy Ghost became the express image of God. This gift of the Holy Ghost was of such value to God that Christ gave His life and blood for it.

It is expedient for you that I go away: for if I go not away, the Comforter [Holy Spirit] will not come unto you; but if I depart, I will send Him unto you.

—JOHN 16:7, EMPHASIS ADDED

Do you understand what Jesus was saying by this? The Holy Spirit given to man was the pinnacle of Christ's work. If we miss this or don't get it quite right in the understanding and experience of it, we have missed the whole thing. We will have missed the *"conclusion"* for the creation of man and the Lord's salvation: God being conceived by the Holy Spirit in our spirit, soul, and body. We are being made one with God in the truest sense, that every atom and substance of our existence would be permeated with the very glory and person of God. Listen to what Peter has to say:

…also a partaker of the glory that shall be revealed.

—1 PETER 5:1

Our bodies become the very body of God, not in philosophical nonsense, but in conscious reality. Moreover, we become full of God, the express image of the Father, Son and Holy Ghost as Christ was! This is where the soul of man sinks back into the "resting place" of His love and joy; His nature, His presence, His being.

My presence shall go with thee, and I will give thee rest.

—EXODUS 33:14

Let's look at an illustration to see what was the first conception of holy matrimony in the mind and heart of God.

THE DIVINE EXCHANGE OF THE TWO TRINITIES

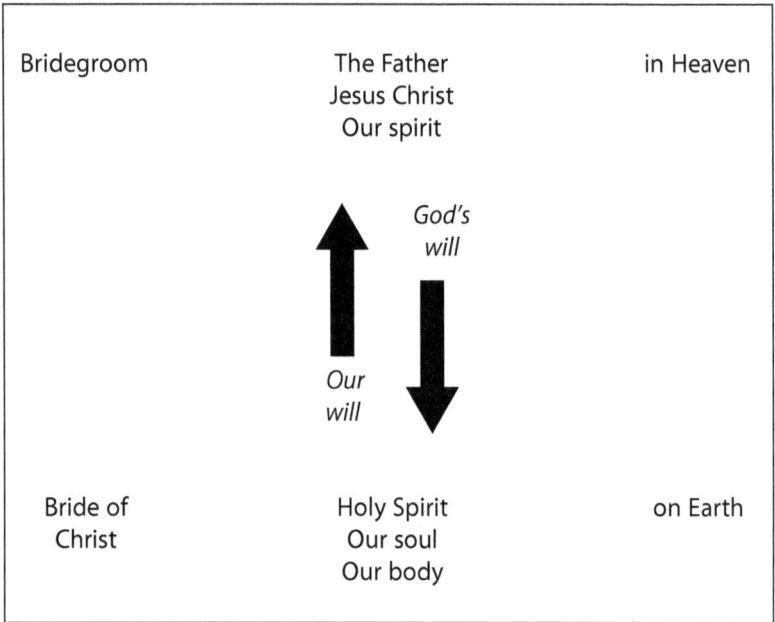

Bridegroom	The Father	in Heaven
	Jesus Christ	
	Our spirit	

God's will

Our will

Bride of	Holy Spirit	on Earth
Christ	Our soul	
	Our body	

John G. Lake with an interpretation of tongues, said: *"Christ is at once the spotless decent of God into man, and the sinless ascent of man into God, and the Holy Ghost is the agent by whom it is accomplished."*[7]

Paul says in Ephesians 2:6:

Made us sit together in heavenly places in Christ Jesus.

Through this marriage the "bride" procreates God in the earth. Moreover the Holy Spirit is God's seal that bars up all the gates and entry points in her and raises up His standard, that she remains sinless and undefiled "lest at any time she dashes her foot against a stone" with no effort of her own. The Holy Spirit is God's seal of the New Covenant and His ring of promise.

Who hath also sealed us, and given the earnest of the Spirit
in our hearts.
—2 Corinthians 1:22

It is by the Holy Spirit taking up residence in man from this divine
union between bride and Bridegroom that the inner man is elevated
to a higher plain of life and existence, and where God's uncreated
Life energy charges every cell within you, quickening you, as Paul
describes:

[God] hath *quickened* us together with Christ...and hath
raised us up together, and made us sit together in heavenly
places in Christ Jesus.
—Ephesians 2:5–6, emphasis added

Let me say that the "name it and claim it" idea has no part in this; i.e.,
the Bible says it therefore I am. If your brother moved to another part of
the country could you say "because he is there so am I"? If you claimed
this reasoning you would soon be found out as living a false life. No, this
event must come down from the throne of God "like a dove" and light
upon you; that you may be lifted up as a bride adorned for her husband,
as a son adopted by his father, not in deception but in *actuality*.

This indeed is the cup that the Lord offers us, in which we will indeed
never thirst again. This is the place of total victory where the kingdom
of darkness is completely annihilated from our lives; receiving His resurrection life, His perfection, His holiness, and our own ascension into
the Godhead. This is the position where we are given the keys of the
kingdom (Matt. 16:19) and exercise complete dominion over the forces
of evil (Eph. 6:12) by the power and authority of the Holy Spirit. It is in
this position that Christ and the Father become incarnate in us and we
truly bear the name Christian, meaning "little Christ." You are offered a
dominion and a fellowship, which Adam and Eve were offered but *never*
saw! Paul knew it:

I should preach among the Gentiles the unsearchable riches
of Christ; and make all men see what is the *fellowship* of

the *mystery*, which from the *beginning* of the world hath been *hid* in God, who created all things by Jesus Christ: to the intent that *now* unto the *principalities and powers in heavenly places* might be *known by the church* the manifold wisdom of God.

—EPHESIANS 3:8–10, EMPHASIS ADDED

The flaming sword (Gen. 3:24) that guarded the mystery of the tree of life has been removed for the church to the intent that we may now understand this fellowship that had been hidden from man until the redemption of Jesus Christ. This gives man the kingdom and dominion as we are lifted into God and seated with Him and He with us (1 John 1:3). Furthermore, because of this fellowship, this divine union with the Godhead through the Holy Spirit, we bear the fruit of His nature effortlessly.

See, this is where carnality has no part in this. An apple tree does not consciously think about bearing apples, it bears apples because that is what it is! If you think that you have to work on bearing God's fruit to produce it, you misunderstand the purpose of God. God bears *Himself* when He moves in! It is God's being that is the rivers of living water that well in our inner man up to eternal life, and flows out into the earth from the center of our person. We become "God-centered" to *glorify* Christ with "greater works" and do *great exploits*, bringing heaven to earth.

Herein is my Father glorified, that ye bear much fruit.

—JOHN 15:8

What is this fruit? The "impossible" to man; the demonstration of the Spirit; the demonstration of His life, His nature and His power in the earth. It is only by this (beyond the socialism of organized religion), that the world comes to know the existence of the living Father, the living Christ, and the living Holy Spirit! It is only by coming into contact with the miraculous life and power of God that the *world* is convicted and convinced, let alone the church, that Jesus Christ is the truth sent by the Father.

It is all through Scripture; Pharaoh came to know the Lord to obey

Him and let the Israelites go; Moses was a type and shadow of God's "sons of glory" to come.

> And thou *shalt be* to him instead of God.
>
> —EXODUS 4:16, EMPHASIS ADDED

The widow at Zaraphath, after Elijah raised up her son from the dead, declared:

> *Now by this* I know that thou art a man of God.
>
> —1 KINGS 17:24, EMPHASIS ADDED

Naaman declared after his leprosy was cleansed:

> *Now I know* that there is no God in all the earth, but in Israel.
>
> —2 KINGS 5:15, EMPHASIS ADDED

Again, Elijah's challenge to the prophets of Baal at Mount Carmel:

> Then the fire of the Lord fell, and consumed the burnt sacrifice, and the wood, and the stones, and the dust, and licked up the water that was in the trench. And when all the people *saw* it, they fell on their faces and they said, "*the* LORD, *He is the God; the* LORD, *He is the God.*"
>
> —1 KINGS 18:38–39, EMPHASIS ADDED

Immediate conversion, just like on the day of Pentecost!

When John sent his disciples to inquire of Jesus if He were the Christ, what did Jesus point them to? His fruit, His works:

> Go and shew John again those things which ye do hear and see: The blind receive their sight, and the lame walk, the lepers are cleansed, and the deaf hear, the dead are raised up, and the poor have the gospel preached to them.
>
> —MATTHEW 11:4–5

Again Jesus says:

> If I do not the works of My Father, *believe Me not.* But if I do, though you believe not Me, believe the *works*: that ye may know, and believe, that the Father is *in Me,* and I *in Him.*
>
> —John 10:37–38, emphasis added

It is by the works, the miraculous, the impossible, the power and authority of God that men are inspired to believe. Jesus was saying, "Look, you don't even have to believe I'm the man of the hour, I'm clothed in flesh like yourselves. But it is by this divine union, this divine marriage within Me by which the fruit, the works that the Father does through Me, flows out, proving My Sonship" (author's paraphrase).

Peter, standing up after receiving the Holy Spirit within, in like manner as Jesus, proclaims:

> Jesus of Nazareth, *a man approved* of God among you *by miracles and wonders and signs,* which *God did* by Him in the midst of you.
>
> —Acts 2:22, emphasis added

This is the only way that God *approves* the Sonship in the spirit of his servants and handmaidens, the rightful heirs to the throne and the keys of the kingdom. The apostles knew this important distinction, when they prayed:

> Grant unto thy servants, that with all boldness they may speak thy word, *by* stretching forth thine hand to heal; and that signs and wonders may be done by the name of they holy child Jesus.
>
> —Acts 4:29–30, emphasis added

Look at this: the speaking of the word and the signs and wonders were inseparable! In fact it was the miraculous that increased their confidence of who they were. Wouldn't it for you?

Consider this: if we look in the dictionary, the definition for *bastard* (which is a lot more then being born out of wedlock), is *"resembling but not typical of the genuine thing."* Also, look up *bastardize*, "to reduce from a higher to a lower state: debase."[8] Isn't this what the majority of Christianity has become, lowering the bar rather than raising it? I mean this with no disrespect, but do we not remain illegitimate children, forging our own path in what seems to be right, by denying the laying down of ourselves? Do we not remain illegitimate by failing to accept the divine union of bride and Bridegroom, that we can be conceived as genuine sons and daughters of the kingdom; that the proof of His life may be wrought through us and we be *approved as children* by miracles signs and wonders? Our lives have moved from being rebellious sinners by the justification of the Lord's blood, but we remain children born out of the wedlock of the new covenant until we are joined as "one" in holy matrimony to God's Spirit; our being joined to His being, our substance joined to His substance, our presence joined to His presence and glory *fusing together* "the new man." Therefore, it becomes His will, power, and person that are exercised through us, proving the *consummation* of the new covenant and the entire restoration of man. Somewhere between justification and glorification the church at large has missed the mark.

Jesus said:

> He that believeth and is *baptized* shall be saved…and these signs shall follow them that believe; in My name shall they cast out devils; they shall speak with new tongues; they shall take up serpents; and if they drink any deadly thing, it shall not hurt them; they shall lay hands on the sick, and they shall recover.
>
> —MARK 16:16–18, EMPHASIS ADDED

What baptism is Jesus talking about? It can't be water baptism, for that is the baptism of repentance (which we all must pass through), nor is water baptism confirmed by the works that Jesus describes here. Therefore He must be referring to the baptism that establishes the *union* between God in man and man in God, through the Holy Spirit. When this heavenly experience takes place in your life and the Holy Spirit takes complete possession and charge of all your faculties, He will govern them by His law of life and bring everything into balance and harmony, making you immune to serpents and poisons and any such thing. It is by these things that God is glorified in us. God declares:

All the earth shall be filled with the glory of the LORD.

—NUMBERS 14:21

How will this be so? By the glorification of you and me.

You are the light of the world.

— MATTHEW 5:14, NKJV

If thy whole body therefore be full of light, having *no part dark*, the whole shall be *full of light*."

—LUKE 11:36, EMPHASIS ADDED

Jesus said:

He that followeth Me shall not walk in darkness, but shall have the *light of life*.

—JOHN 8:12, EMPHASIS ADDED

Jesus is talking about the glorification of man by the presence of the Holy Spirit making His abode within him. The Lord came to restore *every area* of man's life; to free man from sickness, from the oppression of demons and darkness, and to raise him up from "the dead" into His life and glory.

It is in this wise that after giving the apostles power before Pentecost, which was a taste of what was coming, that He commanded them to heal the sick, cleanse the lepers, raise the dead, cast out devils (Matt. 10:8). These were the four areas in which each individual would be set free. Therefore, His *command* was a shadow of man's full salvation in the Holy Spirit; making them ministers of salvation through those four areas, bringing men to the full understanding of what the true children of God must attain to as follows:

- *Heal the sick*: complete deliverance from sickness

- *Cleanse the lepers*: complete deliverance from sin, the nature of sin and every thing that defiles

- *Raise the dead*: filled with the life of Christ in the presence and glory of the Holy Spirit bringing glorification to the individual

- *Cast out devils*: complete deliverance from all darkness and Satan's kingdom

Jesus was the model and the apostles were the proof of this divine union, when the Holy Spirit was poured out. It is absurd to think that anything but a life that *proves* that God and man have been restored whole and one together, joined in glory is the baptism in the Holy Ghost! It is absurd to think that anything but miracles, signs and wonders flowing out as a continual river proves the authenticity of the baptism in the Holy Spirit and approves the genuine child of God! Unfortunately the Lord's church is no longer a living organism inhaling and exhaling the breath of God through this sacred espousal, but a social gathering of commonality with each other (music and fellowship with one another taking preeminence) rather than connection with the living Christ in the power and life born of the Holy Spirit. The church "family" is regarded as proof that we are His, where we help others "feel good" and profit each other's lives. I'm not saying that there is no place for this at all, but this is not *proof*!

It is when this connection to the divine resurrection life of Christ is made that we become kindred with one another and children of the kingdom. This is when we become united as "family" in the truest sense of the Christian meaning. There are those who are hungry and thirsty for the conscious realities of God's kingdom within that are being starved to death without! I pray that what has been said puts your desire on the mark and takes hold of the inheritance of God's true promise. Unwavering faith is the engine that takes us to that real place, out of a pure heart and desire. If every organization that hasn't been planted by God needs to be rooted up and thrown down that the Sons of Glory, the children of God's kingdom be manifested in the earth, so be it. The call is to you, from those chosen to preach the Word to those chosen to serve tables (Acts 6:2–8)! You are called into the mystery of this divine fellowship of God in you that has been hidden from the time of the genetic fall of man; that His presence and nature would flow out of you and that miracles, signs, and wonders would follow you, approving you to be a true child of God. Believe it. Take hold of your destiny now! The fullness of God in you!

Chapter 8

SCRIPTURAL EVIDENCE: WHAT REALLY CHANGED?

WHAT IS ASTONISHING is the *flippancy* with which the term *the baptism in the Holy Spirit* is used, both today and in the writings of the past. It seems to me that if all the baptisms that have been declared were as genuine as those in the days of the Upper Room, Christ would have been surely ushered in by now! We have used the term without the understanding as a whole.

What is even more astonishing is when the baptism in the Holy Spirit is claimed to be received, yet there is no measuring up to the pattern of the apostles, let alone our master Jesus; we pretend what has been received is genuine, when we know in our heart that it is not producing the goods! Why do we do this to ourselves? Why do we choose to live in deception? Why as sheep being led to the slaughter do we remain silent and do not question why the biblical model is not being met? If we stood in a court of law against the evidence of the Bible, accused of *misrepresentation*, would we be found innocent?

Let us examine some of the evidence found in the Bible and see what manifestations are to take place from and around us after the baptism has taken place. In the previous chapters we can begin to understand what life changing events will happen as the purpose of God is manifested in oneself; but now let's look at the biggest *character change* that is to mark every disciple who has truly received.

> When the doors were shut where the disciples were assembled *for fear of the Jews*, came Jesus…
> —JOHN 20:19, EMPHASIS ADDED

The disciples, in other words, were locked inside *themselves,* because of fear. Jesus came and breathed on them to receive the Holy

Spirit and told them to wait for Him (Luke 24:49), which I'm sure they were relieved to hear, since the Jews were in the streets. But lo, when they were all filled with the Holy Spirit, somehow they moved from a private room into the public eye where thousands and thousands of Jews were in the streets of Jerusalem for Pentecost! Peter, who was locked inside like all the rest, stood up and condemned the Jews for killing Jesus. He, along with the rest, became bold, like a light switch had been turned on.

Again Peter, being filled with the Holy Spirit, spake in front of the rulers (Acts 4:8), and the rulers saw the boldness of Peter and John (Acts 4:13). This is the same Peter who could not be associated with Jesus when accused, let alone stand in front of the rulers! Furthermore, they *rejoiced when beaten* because they were counted worthy to suffer for the name of Jesus (Acts 5:41). They also made their stand to obey God in the face of fierce opposition (Acts 5:29). Paul's example is similar:

> And straightway he preached Christ...
>
> —ACTS 9:20

Verses 27–28 testify to him preaching boldly in Jesus's name.

The apostles wore the same bodies but these were clearly not the same people. Their lives were radically changed. They went from one extreme to the other extreme not in a *process*, but in a moment of time! When the Holy Ghost came on them they didn't just throw a welcome mat out the door of the Upper Room and nail a sign on the doorpost reading "All welcome." No! They went out in *fearless confidence and boldness*; this was not only something "given" beyond their natural grasp, but they "knew" that the Holy Spirit had taken possession of them. This is the first character change of a baptized soul.

Second, we also see a great shifting of their motives from "self" to service and obedience solely to the interests of God's kingdom. Thirdly, their actions and motives were overtaken by *love* in a *spirit of unity*. I believe that those gathered in the Upper Room before the Holy Spirit was poured out were there because they shared a *commonality* with each other, and yet were very much *separate individually*, much like we see today. They were there in one accord "*doing*" the same thing, which was offering up prayer and supplication. But after they were filled, scripture records in Acts 4:32 that the multitude of them that believed were of "one heart and of one soul and had all things common." This was clearly a work of the Spirit that they had not achieved on their own. They went from striving to be the "greatest" individually to serving one another; they were no longer separate from each other, but one. This is not to be confused with the human affection of the soul wanting the feeling of "family community." No, this is far beyond that.

Other evidences that are to become regular occurrences are found in Joel 2:28–29 which Peter quoted. They are *prophetic utterances, visions and dreams*. These were given to help, encourage, warn and direct the church in God's work. We see in Acts many examples of this. Ananias was given instructions what to do concerning Paul in a vision, and Paul was shown what to expect by a vision (Acts 9:10, 12). Peter, in a trance, was given insight into God's purpose through a vision, which was the opening for the Gentiles (Acts 10:10). Stephen had seen an open vision of the Lord and saw Him standing at the right hand of God to encourage him at the end of his life (Acts 7:56). Paul received a night vision (which could also mean a dream) and was instructed to go to Macedonia (Acts 16:9). Again, in a night vision the Lord encouraged Paul to speak in the place he was staying (Acts 18:9–10). Agabus, a certain prophet from Judaea, gave warning to Paul through a prophetic utterance (Acts 21:10–11); he also gave warning to the church about a great famine (Acts 11:28).

The Holy Spirit was also communicating to them directly. He *told* Peter to go with the three men, doubting nothing (Acts 10:20). The Holy Spirit *forbade* them to preach the word in Asia (Acts 16:6), and gave direction saying, "Separate unto Me Barnabas and Paul" (Acts 13:2). He *told* Philip to join himself to the eunuch's chariot (Acts 8:29).

They could discern the thoughts and intents of the heart, just as Jesus knew what the people were thinking. We see this in Acts 5:1–11 when Ananias and Sapphira stood before Peter and lied about the money they received for the sale of their land. And the power of Peter's rebuke produced such conviction in their hearts they fell down dead. These works caused true godly fear in the people, which the Bible describes as *great* fear. It was seen and testified to in the lives of all of them, and produced a reverence for Almighty God that is not even understood today, let alone experienced.

The apostles' eyes were opened to the spirit world as well, that they could see and receive help by God's ministering spirits, the angels (Heb.1:14). Philip received his instruction by the mouth of an angel (Acts 8:26). Paul was encouraged by an angel to "Fear not" and given instruction about the saving of all aboard the ship (Acts 27:23). An angel of the Lord was sent to assist Peter's escape from prison (Acts 12:7).

Translation became possible also. Philip, being caught up in the spirit, was taken from one place to another (Acts 8:39–40). Paul was caught up in the spirit and taken to paradise, not knowing whether he was in his body at the time or not (2 Cor. 12:4). *These are all proof that the Lord was working with them* (Mark 16:20)!

Now let's look at what Jesus Himself said:

> I will pray the Father, and he shall give you another Comforter, that He may abide with you for ever; even the spirit of truth…ye know Him; for He dwelleth *with* you [now] and *shall be in* you [later].
>
> —John 14:16–17, emphasis added

> The Comforter, which is the Holy Ghost, whom the Father will send in My name, He shall teach you all things, and bring all things to your remembrance, whatsoever I have said unto you.
>
> —John 14:26

> When the Comforter is come…He shall testify of Me.
>
> —John 15:26

When He the Spirit of Truth, is come, He will guide you into all truth: for He shall not speak of Himself; but whatsoever He shall hear, that shall He speak: and He will [show] you things to come. He shall glorify Me: for He shall receive of Mine, and shall [show] it unto you.

—JOHN 16:13–14, EMPHASIS ADDED

The time cometh, when I shall no more speak unto you in proverbs, but I shall [show] you plainly of the Father.

—JOHN 16:25, EMPHASIS ADDED

If any man thirst, let him come unto Me, and drink. He that believeth on Me, as the Scripture hath said, out of his belly shall flow rivers of living water.

—JOHN 7:37–38

In these verses Jesus is telling us what will happen.

These signs shall *follow* them that believe; in my name shall they cast out devils; they shall speak with new tongues; they shall take up serpents; and if they drink any deadly thing, it shall not hurt them; they shall lay hands on the sick, and they shall recover.

—MARK 16:17–18, EMPHASIS ADDED

Verily, verily I say unto you, He that believeth on Me, the works that I do shall he do also; and *greater works* than these shall he do; because I go unto My Father.

—JOHN 14:12, EMPHASIS ADDED

Here Jesus is making claims as to what we will do. In both cases Jesus is laying out markers to the claims of receiving the Holy Spirit. But by the words out of Christ's *own* mouth there is only *one* evidence, I repeat, *only one* that can be *directly linked* as evidence to the event of the baptism in the Holy Spirit initially and ongoing.

> Ye shall *receive power, after that* the Holy Ghost is come
> upon you.
>
> —Acts 1:8, emphasis added

If everything else was thrown out of court, it is Christ's words that would not fail. Paraphrasing what Jesus said, "You shall receive power, first; when you do receive that power, after that you will know that the Holy Ghost is come upon you." Jesus is saying there is *absolutely no question* that the Holy Spirit has come when you have received this power. If the church *riveted their minds and hearts* on what the Lord determines the "proof" to be, the world would be turned upside down!

Why was this the most important evidence in the Lord's mind?

> Ye shall be *witnesses* unto Me. [Locally and to all the earth.]
>
> —Acts 1:8, emphasis added

But witnesses to what?

> With great power gave the apostles *witness of the resurrection of the Lord Jesus.*
>
> —Acts 4:33, emphasis added

It is this power that proves to the world that Jesus is the living Son of God, the Savior of the world, and we are to be His ministers. So, what is this power? The Greek word used by Jesus to declare, "Ye shall receive *power*," is the same word found in the Gospel accounts that use the English word "*virtue.*"

> And Jesus, immediately knowing in Himself that *virtue*
> [means power in Greek] had gone out of Him…
>
> —Mark 5:30, emphasis added

> And the whole multitude sought to touch Him: for there
> went *virtue* [means power in Greek] out of Him, and healed
> them all.
>
> —Luke 6:19, emphasis added

And Jesus said, Somebody hath touched Me: for I perceive that *virtue* [means power in Greek] is gone out of Me.

—LUKE 8:46, EMPHASIS ADDED

Jesus commands the disciples to:

Tarry ye in the city of Jerusalem, until ye be endued with *power* from on high.

—LUKE 24:49, EMPHASIS ADDED

Again, the word *power* used here is synonymous in the Greek with the English word virtue in the previous verses. Also, the definition for the word *endued* in English and the literal Greek means to be "clothed" as with a garment. You can understand the symbolism when Elijah cast his mantle upon Elisha (1 Kings 19:19). The Lord was using Elijah's mantle to show us the clothing of His power upon us. Indeed, this is the mantle we need.

Therefore, Jesus is saying that this very same *power* that clothed Me will clothe you! Power as currents of electricity described by John G. Lake and Charles Finney. Power that can be perceived, or that your senses are aware of abiding upon you and flowing out through you. Power that "healed them all" and did the Father's work would rest on you.

This is the same power by which Peter stood up with confidence and declared "*This is that which was spoken of*" (Acts 2:16, emphasis added), and Peter's testimony to the lame man, "*such as I have, I give to thee*" (Acts 3:6, emphasis added); a power that was the overwhelming witness beyond a shadow of doubt that the Holy Spirit was possessing them.

Although the Holy Spirit clothing the disciples in power on the day of Pentecost is not specifically mentioned in the second chapter of Acts, the surmounting proof of this is laid out in no uncertain terms as the *genuine evidence* spoken by Christ to His disciples in Acts 1:8. And by understanding the events recorded in the book of Acts as a whole we can safely assume that Christ's words were definitely fulfilled.

Therefore, what results are recorded? The first evidence of this is the power to convict and convert souls to Christ.

> Now when they heard this, they were pricked in their heart.
>
> —ACTS 2:37

> The same day there were added unto them about three thousand souls.
>
> —ACTS 2:41

Again:

> Howbeit, many of them which heard the word believed; and the number of the men was about five thousand.
>
> —ACTS 3:4

Charles Finney testifies that after being endued with this power, just a few words to someone produced conviction, and every word he spoke seemed to be accompanied by the power of the Holy Spirit.[1]

Secondly, they did indeed fulfill the words of Jesus, and signs and wonders *immediately* followed them as declared in Acts 2:43. Take note that this did not just happen to twelve people; *all 120* disciples received with Peter as he pronounced:

> The promise is unto you, and to your children, and to all that are afar off, even as many as the LORD our God shall call.
>
> —ACTS 2:39

We really have to recognize and grasp that from the moment of the baptism of the Holy Spirit in Acts 2:4 there was a *continual progression* of events; only increasing, never decreasing, and it didn't stop!

> And by the hands of the apostles were many signs and wonders wrought among the people.
>
> —ACTS 5:12

Insomuch that they brought for the sick into the streets, and laid them on beds and couches, that at the least the shadow of Peter passing by might overshadow some of them. There came also a multitude out of the cities round about unto Jerusalem, bringing sick folks, and them which were vexed with unclean spirits: and they were healed every one.

—ACTS 5:15–16

They were healed, everyone, by the *same power* that was given to Jesus! The question the disciples asked in the Gospels, "why couldn't we cast him out?" became irrelevant. They moved beyond their limit to God's limit.

Stephen, called to the daily ministration of serving tables, a common "waiter" and not a preacher:

…full of faith and power, did great wonders and miracles among the people.

—ACTS 6:8

The people listened to Philip and gave heed to his words:

Hearing and seeing the miracles which he did. For unclean spirits, crying with loud voice, came out of many that were possessed with them: and many taken with palsies, and that were lame, were healed.

—ACTS 8:6–7

Peter raised Dorcas from the dead, and "presented her alive" (Acts 9:40–41). Then we see Paul after the *initial* Pentecost, *"one who was born out of due time"* (1 Cor. 15:8), receive the *same power* and perform the *same* miracles, signs, and wonders. And the word confirms that Paul and Barnabas were "granted signs and wonders to be done by their hands" (Acts 14:3).

Paul healed a crippled man from birth (Acts 14:8–10)

> And God wrought special miracles by the hands of Paul: so
> that from his body were brought unto the sick handkerchiefs
> or aprons, and the diseases departed from them, and the
> evil spirits went out of them.
>
> —Acts 19:11–12

In contrast to these things, the evil spirit answered the sons of Sceva when they tried to expel a demon:

> Jesus *I know*, and Paul *I know*; but who are ye?
>
> —Acts 19:15, emphasis added

So how did the evil spirit know Jesus and Paul? *By this power and authority upon them!*

> And they were all amazed, and spake among themselves,
> saying, What word is this! For with authority and power
> He commandeth the unclean spirits, and they come out.
>
> —Luke 4:36

Paul on the island of Melita was unaffected by the venomous snake that fastened onto his hand (Acts 28:3–5). And he healed the island's people who suffered from sickness and disease (Acts 28:8–9).

With this mountain of evidence of power from on high staring us in the face pertaining to the true baptism in the Holy Spirit for the believer, how can we be found guiltless in this matter? Are we afraid to question these things because the "Romans will come and take away our place and nation"? Or are we afraid that if we question, the very foundation of our belief system will come under scrutiny, and if the truth is known all that we know will come to an end? Are we afraid to question because it may cause us to reconsider what the definition of a believer is, and therefore require us to make new choices? Or maybe if we questioned we would lose our hierarchical position and power somewhere. It all comes down to what we hold more dearly, and what we truly desire. Change never comes without the embracing of hard questions and careful investigation.

These were more noble than those in Thessalonica, in that they received the word with all readiness of mind, and searched the Scriptures daily, whether those things were so.

—Acts 17:11

We cannot serve the "ideal" Christian life and ignore what a true witness of the resurrection is. Nor can we bury our lack of "clothing in power" under a cloak of church goings, doings or services. In light of these things let us not stiffen our necks, but humble our obstinate hearts. Let us pray with all our might for God to give His power and glory to us and to the church no matter what the cost, that we can prove to the world that Jesus Christ is alive by the *"very works' sake"*!

Chapter 9

THE WAR DIALOGUE: A LOOK AT THE OTHER SIDE

N EWS WAS TRICKLING down the corridors of hell the day God blew His Spirit and fire into the Upper Room on Pentecost.

"There's dreadful news lord Satan." The chief messenger sat there trembling.

"Legions and legions of our army left their territory."

"What! What is the meaning of this?"

Satan swung around to look at him and grabbed him by the throat.

"You don't…you don't understand, they, they were driven out," he heaved. The demon barely choked it out.

"They had no chance to retaliate."

His eyes grew wider as he was engulfed by Satan and then dropped to the ground.

"Why?" Satan demanded.

"The Holy Father sent His Spirit to Jesus's followers."

"Why, why, what does that matter? He was with them before, and that never bothered us. Peter was a case in point: he was wonderfully filled with my fear and unbelief when Jesus needed him the most."

"No, no, this is different. The Holy Spirit seems to have entered into them just as we do. The brightness of His glory and presence has left our army without a shadow of darkness to hide behind. They were defenseless against His light."

"How can this be? They all have the nature of me within them from the fall of Adam." Lowering himself back into his seat, Satan began musing.

"They were born with it. The seed of sin! They've all been tainted! God wouldn't breach His judgment to live in man! I stopped His plan with Adam and Eve!" he crowed triumphantly.

"Y-ye-yes, b-bu-but, now Jesus's death satisfied the Father's judgment for man and..."

"And what? I know all this!" Satan said, rising swiftly from his throne.

"Well, well we saw that when His Spirit came He sent with Him fire from the altar and burnt up everything that was left from Adam, even their weaknesses we used to indulge in," he whined. "I don't know what we're going to do, now these people are completely out of our control."

"Do you know what this means?" He began pacing back and forth.

"They have become exactly what I have fought to destroy since the creation of man!" he screeched. *"This means they've become like the Most High, just as Jesus was. I thought that this would be the end of God's plan the second time by killing His Christ, but now the problem has become worse."*

"I agree my lord, it has been reported that God has now taken His royal seal and placed it at each one of their entry points; we no longer have access to them on the inside. We have had enough trouble trying to divert people from the truth when Jesus was on earth, what are we going to do now that the Father's holy seed has been multiplied?"

"Right now we have only one choice. We must raise up every religious spirit we have with a vengeance in all those we have convinced not to believe in Jesus. We'll send forth murder into their hearts and kill these miserable wretches with horrible deaths to make others think twice about believing in the Christ. After they're all dead we will take control of the land through religious tradition once again. Double up the hordes in their ranks; Deceit, Lies, and Half-truth, to march under the banner of Religion! We must be even more diligent than ever. This is the greatest threat to my kingdom. For if we let this get out of hand the end will surely come. Where there is life, we will breathe death. Where there is health, we will breathe disease. Where there is love, we will breathe hate. Where there is unity, we will breathe forth division!"

"Yes, but surely people will read history and God will draw them to know."

"Huh, we will make this Christ of God as dead and cold as the Arctic snow in the minds of His followers. He will be just another lifeless religion when I'm through with Him. I will see to it that this provision is stamped out with my pomp and pride. It will become just another rule of the day. I may not be able to hold Him in chains here, but that is where He will be held in the minds of His people! Call the hordes in, let's prepare for this war!"

19TH TO 20TH CENTURY

"Lord Satan, there are some who the Father is drawing to read the history of that dreadful day when He took possession of Jesus's early disciples and drove us out. These selected ones believe that they can receive Him as well."

"Well you know what to do. Do whatever it takes to keep them in disobedience and into the pleasures of life. If there is one whose faith is too strong for us and breaks through, we will make that one out to be a god, holier than the rest, whose followers we will make to worship. Then, divide and isolate them from the rest of Christ's wretches, making their god to be the truth."

"What happens if a group does break through? Times have changed, we can no longer openly kill."

"We will send out mocking and blasphemy to keep it from spreading into controlled territory. Then we will deceive their followers into accepting something far less, giving them at the same time pleasure and pride of mind, thinking they have the full extent of what we have witnessed that first loathsome Pentecost. This will keep our territory and puff them up so when someone brings them the truth they will reject it. Continuing this strategy, the rest of Christ's wretches and our beloved in the world will discredit their experiences as useless; then we will use them as proof that Christ doesn't display any real power or authority in the earth through them. Go, take these orders to the front lines."

Jesus was in such a state of being that by the power and presence of the Holy Spirit possessing Him, He was impenetrable. There was absolutely no stopping Him in Satan's ranks. He was the most destructive force to Satan's kingdom in human form. Do we think of Jesus as our master? What did Jesus tell us?

The disciple is not above his master: but every one that is perfect *shall be as his master.*

—LUKE 6:40, EMPHASIS ADDED

This isn't a promise. This is a fact. Do you believe in Christ? Again He said:

Verily, verily, I say unto you, he that believeth on Me, the works that I do shall he do also; and *greater works than these shall he do*; because I go unto My Father.

—JOHN 14:12, EMPHASIS ADDED

Again He tells us:

Ye shall receive power, after that the Holy Ghost is come upon you.

—ACTS 1:8

Now we know in the book of Acts the disciples did indeed receive the fulfillment of these words as discussed in the previous chapter and became a multiplied *Jesus,* marked by the same destructive force against Satan's kingdom. Don't you think that if the promise of the Holy Spirit and His power is the most destructive weapon against the devil, he will use everything in his power and government to stop it? Absolutely, he will! I tell you the truth: there is not one single thing more threatening or terrifying to all hell than an individual receiving this unadulterated event of the Holy Spirit and power. If there is a hit list against the truths of God this is number one!

Awake! Awake! Think! Think! If you were a soldier in a war against your enemy and somewhere out there, there was a weapon with such destructive force that you could wipe him off the face of the map, don't you think the biggest part of the war for the enemy would be to keep you from it at all costs? It would be foolish to think otherwise. The enemy knows you are powerless without it and can hold you at a defensive position on the front line. But with it the tables are turned, and he is rendered powerless and on the defensive run himself!

Look at the nuclear arms race in the world. This is the biggest threat to humanity because of the power of these bombs. Whichever country packs the biggest punch first can hold the others at its mercy. The one who achieves this has the power behind them to speak words and make the biggest threats and demands with the control being in their favor. The same is true in the spirit world. The Holy Ghost and His power is our nuclear bomb. The devil will use every deceptive trick in his bag to blind your eyes from this, keeping you on the defensive; always battling, always warring, and making you think you're fighting the good fight of faith, when really the truth is you're hanging on by your fingernails, close to defeat. Yet somewhere in some field lies the most powerful destructive weapon waiting silently to be unearthed. Should we not sell all and buy that field?

Chapter 10

STOPPING SHORT

I N THIS CHAPTER I want to touch on some things that may be holding back the body of Christ. There is a misconception when it comes to "soaking," or waiting for God's presence. Waiting on God is most definitely biblical, "those who wait upon the Lord shall renew their strength" (Isa. 40:31) and a discipline we should all learn. Furthermore, the Lord speaks to His people in this way. This can bring great times of refreshing, therefore the practice itself is correct, but to come and wait for God's presence to manifest itself to you, should only at most be a means to an end. This would be considered "a taste."

> Taste and see that the LORD is good.
>
> —PSALM 34:8

Your destiny is having God's presence remaining in you. One may say "I do have God's presence in me." Let me be frank, if you are seeking God each day to have a daily "touch" from the throne you do not really know His continual abiding presence within, insomuch that you are so full of God that seeking ceases and resting begins, hunger and thirst are satisfied. As Jesus said, drink of this water and you will never thirst again.

So why is there so much thirsting for "another" touch from God? The Godhead's desire is to manifest their glory within you, for you to be glorified with Christ. Why do we continue to seek what Moses sought for, that which never abides or remains? We can become dependent on a fading glory. This is not your destiny as a believer. Under the old covenant Moses sought the Lord *Show me your glory*" (Exod. 33:18, NKJV). In the same way, this is what we ask of the Lord when we wait for His presence, "show me your glory." But we are not living under the old covenant but the new. Therefore, the euphoric state or illumination or even encounters with God's heavenly host we may experience are not to be the end result, but to draw us closer to the reservoir of life. Although this may be a pinnacle in our growth it is merely a plateau between the base of the mountain and the peak. Christ's victory on the cross bought us the privilege to seek God's indwelling presence through the person of the Holy Spirit. Therefore, your destiny through Christ is for His glory and presence to dwell with and in you 24–7, now and forever; being fully prepared in season and whatever season. Why do we not allow ourselves to conceive the thought that God wants us to experience His glory and presence perpetually, ongoing, never ending, glorifying us with Himself, that we in turn may glorify Him!

Let us not be deceived by the fact that we have seen God move in our lives in certain ways and hold to that method. If we are not moving toward our glorification through His continual abiding presence within us, we are not possessing our Canaan. If we have trouble with the thought that God wants us to be *identical* to Christ it is only because we are still "slaves coming out of Egypt", looking at ourselves rather than God's promise. The disciples were coined "little Christs" i.e., Christians, because that is what they displayed. We have become so weighted down with subconscious mind-sets like "once a sinner always a sinner," that we couldn't possibly think of being "like" God as a son or daughter is like their parent. We focus on our inabilities rather than the Father's provision through Christ's victory, through Christ's blood.

We are blameless through the Lord's blood, but I'm convinced that our justification is only set up for us so that we are given space to repent and come under the obedience to His promised baptism in the Holy Spirit fire and power to the cleansing, keeping, and complete restoration of our whole being. The understanding that we need to draw out of the Lord's words to the Laodicean church in Revelation 3:14–22 is this: we have become comfortably lukewarm in the doctrine of justification, with the sense of God's richness in it. But Christ says, "Do you not know what a little way you have come?" So we must be rebuked and chastened to see our nakedness. Jesus goes on to describe in verses

18 and 20 the glorification of Himself in us through the work of the Holy Spirit.

Therefore, if we are hanging around the corridors of justification seeking "touches" from God (as good as they might be, and God indeed is patient and merciful with us), we are grieving the Holy Spirit by not fervently setting our faces to take our fellowship from a meeting with God to becoming "ONE" with Him as Jesus prayed for those who believed would receive (John 17:20–23); a never-fading presence or lessening glory abiding in us. I'm not saying that this experience eliminates spending intimate time alone with God; Jesus spent time with the Father all night after He was reunited with Him through the person of the Holy Spirit. I'm also not saying that you will not seek God over various issues as did the apostles when they entreated the Lord to give them greater boldness to speak His Word, and that signs would be done in the name of His Holy child Jesus, which resulted in the room being shaken. But, the purpose moves this fellowship with God into an entirely different dimension of continually being in His presence, which is the Father's heart for His children.

∽

Another issue that demands our attention similar to the one already mentioned is working for God with spiritual results. What I mean by this is that God gives each person gifts according to every person's ability and calling (1 Peter 4:11), to be ministered in God's "economy" (Luke 19:15).

God's gifts are given without repentance, meaning that they are given and *not* to be taken back. Here is where the deception of the gifts comes in. As one ministers his or her gift or gifts and finds success, the person is liable to *stop short* of God's full salvation, or *fall* from grace entirely in this stage of growth. The gifts are only the first fruits and given while in a state of justification, therefore, the carnal nature is still *alive*. In this state the flesh can begin to rule these gifts, and this is very much the enemy's intent. By this, the one ministering becomes deluded into thinking that God is "with them" no matter what he or she does, straying from the truth, subtle as it may be. A perfect example of this in Scripture is that of King Solomon.

> For it came to pass, when Solomon was old, that his wives
> turned away his heart after other gods: and *his heart was*
> *not perfect* with the LORD his God, as was the heart of
> David his father.
>
> —1 KINGS 11:4, EMPHASIS ADDED

In 1 Kings 3:12–13, God gave Solomon wisdom, more so than any other, as well as riches and honor above all other kings in the earth. How is it that Solomon could go after other gods when he received so much? The answer is simple. At the height of his power and the "flowing" of his gift of wisdom, he didn't consider his heart! Solomon's gift from God, which did not cease (because God gave it to him without repentance), deceived him.

When he began to go after strange gods and drift away from God's commandments, he must have sat in his throne and conceived in his mind, "I must be on the right track for my gift is still operating through me." The flowing of a gift can never be used as a sign to confirm the "rightness" of our heart or actions. When God has given a gift to someone, it becomes *a part of them*, to match the person's personality and what they were designed and destined for.

Your gift therefore is *not directly correlated with your heart*. I will not name names, but if you study people from the past whom God gifted tremendously, when they disobeyed and turned their heart away and not followed perfectly, their gifting still operated. But God had to remove them from their position, just as He stirred up those around Solomon.

See, God's interest is not your gifts. His interest is your heart, that you seek His full salvation in Christ, to the cleansing and glorification of your entire being through the Holy Spirit; He wants you to be changed into the nature and identity of Christ, that you become the giver of God, not your gift; then God becomes the *possessor of your gift*, to be enhanced, elevated, and ministered out. So why the gifts in the first place? When you start a new job you begin in a certain area for which you become responsible. In the same way, God gives you something to be responsible for and faithful with; through this you are proving your trustworthiness. Also, the gifts are there to give you the opportunity to submit, yield, and obey. These qualities are necessary for God to take possession of you as you seek His fullness. This is your ultimate destiny, that you become fully apprehended by God; this should continue to be your focus until you receive this, *not your gifts*. Your gifts are only to be traded along the lines of proving yourself to God. We must press into God's best, His purpose for man, and His completeness for us. Therefore, even the highly demonstrative gifts like healing and miracles are in the end of little value to the minister who has been given them, if the hunger and thirst stops short of receiving the pearl of great price, the merging of man into God and God into man. Moreover, we can clearly understand from this the Lord's words:

> Not every one that saith unto me, Lord, Lord, shall enter into the kingdom of heaven; but he that doeth the will of my Father which is in heaven. Many will say to me in that day, Lord, Lord, have we not prophesied in thy name? and in thy name done many wonderful works? And then will I profess unto them, I never knew you: depart from me, ye that work iniquity.
>
> —Matthew 7:21–23

Remember Judas; he was "gifted" along with all the other disciples and performed the same wonderful works as they. Judas received that which was without repentance and it remained with him. Now consider this real possibility. On his way to betray Jesus it was *solely within his possession* to have healed a few sick folk or cast out some devils! Do you see the point?

On the *surface* the "wonderful works" certainly look like the Father's will, but the fact of the matter, which we established in the previous chapters, is that the Father's will is the total restoration of man individually. That man is lifted to a higher holy life without sin, through the atmosphere of heaven descending into man by the presence and power of the Holy Spirit. This is God's true gift, which Judas did not take part in.

I believe that misunderstanding God's mind and purpose here is what allows a fleshly hierarchy to be built within the church. Each person receives their appropriate gift and one is more "exciting" than the other, and the exaltation of man lifts up one above another; envy and competition come in with strife and debate, and this becomes the foundation for church politics. The people are crying out, "We will have a king to reign over us." What needs to be grasped is that *all believers* are to possess God, and His power is to be upon everyone. By this divine fellowship in the Spirit of God, *all* are to live and experience the miraculous.

All are given, through this fullness of God in man, the power to heal the sick, cleanse the lepers, raise the dead, and cast out devils. This is the common place of every worker in Christ by the clothing of power upon each one. There would be no competition in such a body as this, and then each person's specific gifts would fit to hold everything together, while God holds onto us, keeping us from falling.

◇

Third is the idea of self-deliverance. Although we are given authority through Jesus's name and are in warfare with the enemy and need to be aware of the wiles of the devil, some people have embraced self-deliverance as a *lifestyle*. They tout it as the new truth to becoming "more free," or a path to staying free, possibly neglecting weightier biblical principals that form character and the direction that God intends as an end result. Therefore, they can become like spiritual watchdogs, always on the defensive guard for the next time the slightest thing happens, and a door is opened for the devil from the "trauma." If the devil can achieve drawing our attention to the slightest misfortunes, he will throw all kinds of problems at us to keep us going around and around in a circle. The very fact that our "attention" is devil-ward is a door in itself.

I'm not saying that there are not times when the devil needs to be confronted. But on the extreme end, self-deliverance can become a life lived in *continual exhausting warfare*! Do I suggest people have not seen something take place through self-deliverance? Not at all. I have read of successful cases and believe they are true and I don't discredit any victory someone can or has received, but this really is not the point at hand. I do suggest that on the whole the practice can get a person into a rut. Satan would like to cover up the main objective God has for us in what it truly means to be "free" and be *constantly kept* in his "arena."

In the pursuit of God, self-deliverance can become a trap for many people if they have "parked their car here." When we accept Christ and believe that He is the Son of God we are given access to call on His name "Jesus Christ" and His grace for help; and the authority of that name against the enemy. The Lord may even take us through a season of relying on His name *only* for spiritual growth; I am not ruling any possibility out, but that season (as all seasons do) comes to an end, as we grow closer to Him. Like justification this is given to get us through to *maturity*! Please don't get me wrong, I'm not saying that calling on the Lord's name will cease, for it is by His name that He receives the Glory; but we can get used to a method, missing the point of where we need to get to.

For example, when one enlists into his nation's army, he is given a uniform and given access to things to help him in his training to become *higher in rank*. At the beginning he has no more than his fellow privates, but he does have more than the general public. If there was a threat from the enemy he could go to the commanding officer and receive the authority to deal with the enemy. But as he advances in position he becomes more like the commanding officer, not left on the defensive, but commanding the victory.

Nevertheless, the Scriptures do not teach self-deliverance or this method whatsoever; but by our closeness to God, purity of heart, willingness to repent and change and our obedience to His voice and will for our lives, deliverance comes. As the Lord spoke to Moses, if the Israelites would listen, keep and do His judgments, then *God would* take away from them all sickness, and put none of the evil diseases of Egypt upon them (Deut. 7:15). Time and again, if they repented and turned from their wicked ways, God would repent of the evil He was bringing upon them. When Hezekiah was sick and dying, he prayed and wept very hard, and the Lord healed him and added fifteen years to his life.

On the other hand, our "traumas" or mishaps may very well be the grounds by which we are sifted like wheat, working in us a far greater work than trying to cut them off in Jesus's name. Those who have become solid leaders with faces like flint have been made wise in understanding this. God's motive for every believer is not that we wield His name like a spiritual shotgun hoping to hit our target, but that our human nature is melted like wax, making way for a greater work of His Spirit within.

This leads me to my next point: we can continually cast things out, but if our *attitude and character* remain the same, are we really getting to the "deliverance" God desires? We could war against the devil in this fashion and completely avoid our character issues God wants to deal with. Why would the Lord only want us delivered up to a certain point? Of course He wants to take us entirely out of the pigpen that we are no longer frolicking with the swine. But it may be in God's wisdom that as we do things God's way, steadily moving forward in our lives, that the enemy will be driven off the land bit by bit, especially if the wild beasts of old habits and an unrenewed mind still prevail in our character. We need to understand God's heart for full restoration and completeness, with which we can become completely free.

As we humble ourselves and submit to God first, resisting the nature of the temptation, deliverance comes (James 4:6–8). Come close to God and God will come close to you. How? Cleanse your hands and purify your hearts. Since my own conversion there has been no other method applied to my life that brought me deliverance. Some things just dropped off because of my love and passion for God. Others took resistance, but whatever it was, it was simply broken in the end. If we are in constant conflict over something in our lives, it is usually because of unwillingness to change on the whole, in character or in obedience to God's Word and will; we are in bondage. If we are clean before God and walking in His truth, or at least continually moving towards that, He puts up a hedge of protection around us as described in the life of Job; even Satan acknowledged this (Job 1:9–10). Can we not expect the same? I believe we can, and should. It is the devil who would want us to believe otherwise.

Let's go a little deeper with this. The epitome of the religious spirit is focusing on oneself; self-deliverance, self-renunciation, self-chastisement, (I am talking in the extreme sense) all fall under choosing one's own cross to bear. When Jesus said, "Deny thyself," He did not mean to focus on "self," but rather to be completely focused on Him. By looking to Christ with all that we are, will in fact, *dissolve self*! That is the true essence of self-denial. If it were Christ's mind to have the disciples "clean" themselves and focus on setting themselves free, why did He not lay out this pattern for us in the word?

Take, for example, when the disciples argued amongst themselves who would be the greatest. Jesus didn't exhort them that they needed to deliver themselves from a spirit of pride, although it was there. When Peter was gripped with fear at the arrest and trial of Jesus, Jesus did not say, "When thou hast these things arise within you, I say unto you, deliver thyself"!

One may point to Ephesians 6:12, "For we wrestle not against flesh and blood." This is clearly a passage that is meant to deal with the devil without and not within. In 2 Corinthians 12:7 Paul was given a thorn in the flesh, a messenger from Satan to buffet him. What does Paul do? He prays that God would deal with the "thorn." It is fruitless to think that we can set ourselves free from six thousand years of demonic activity and inherited wickedness through our generations with the complexity of it all. Man was not purposed to take on such a task, nor was it in the heart of God that we should focus on the devil like this in our daily lives and devote countless hours to "freeing" ourselves. This is not the definition of salvation and victory, but greater bondage! This method has the tendency to sidetrack us from complete submission and surrender to God regarding the issues that really need to be dealt with in our lives. This is the real reason why we remain in bondage in the first place, not because we haven't waged good enough warfare.

Furthermore, are we just trying to get free from the devil and not get free from our own corrupt selves, where open doors are created *for* the devil? Trying to deliver ourselves from the devil will never happen, even if we were given all eternity to do it; we cannot in our own strength (even if we are using the Lord's name) close the revolving door on the corrupt inherited nature written into us, which allows the devil access within. This is where the real problem lies. Therefore, if you can't free yourself from the root of the tree, cutting off its branches is futile.

These *issues* that were in the disciples did not *disturb* Jesus. He knew what was the root in man; He knew what was in his members. What was stemming forth from them was "par for the course," it was a "normal" outcome under the circumstances. Christ was leading them to His plan of full salvation, full restoration, where they would find complete, everlasting deliverance and victory from the devil within. He was preparing them to yield their hearts to God, to receive His consuming fire and the presence and power of the Holy Spirit within them.

Everything unclean and dark from the fall of man would be driven out at the coming of God's glorious light, love, and being. His ultimate hedge, His seal, would be placed within you bringing a total and complete transformation in one instantaneous moment, never battling with self or Satan on the inside again! You will have become God's possession, under His control and command. Glorious! Jesus said, "All of us who are weary and heavy laden" come to Him and He will give us rest. This is not a rest that we would have to make up or pretend, but a promise to be taken hold of with unrelenting faith.

God's glory is promised to fill your tabernacle (2 Peter 1:13–14), driving out all wickedness and setting you completely free, because the devils and darkness cannot "comprehend the light" (John 1:5). The only focus God intended us to heed is to receive God Himself into us. From this point our lives become caught up in His River of Life; He takes dominion for us within and we take dominion for Him without. Smith Wigglesworth says, "By the power of the Spirit, as God gives us revelation, be lifted up into a very blessed state of fellowship with God, of power with God. And in that place of power with God, we will have power over everything else."[1] This is Christian maturity! Let us stand still, take hold of God, and watch His salvation.

∼

Last, there is a real deception when people don't see their total depravity, let alone think that anything can be done about it. On a subconscious level, they know that they are completely powerless to stop such a corrupt nature; therefore, the conscious mind does not struggle, but accepts defeat and conveys to the individual that, "This is *who I am.*" Then there is the other side, equally deceptive for the individual, that does see their total depravity and in their own strength tries to correct it.

The idea that one can practice the fruits of the Spirit and work these virtues into his or her life is preposterous! I agree that the will of a person is very strong, and when one sets their *willpower* to achieve such virtues he or she can do so; but only to the same degree that they suppress their own fallen nature (which is in fact *using* their fallen nature or soul life to produce such results). But the state of the person is not truly dealt with on the inside.

D.L. Moody states, "The great trouble with many is that they are trying to make these graces. They are trying to create love; they are to make peace; they are trying to manufacture joy. But these are creatures of human planting. To produce them of ourselves is impossible. That is an act of God. They come from above."[2]

People may learn habits by forcing themselves to take actions that show forth love to others. I do think we should be as kind as we can be in the intern while we move on; therefore, I'm not suggesting that we let our carnal nature reign totally unchecked. In fact, positive actions like these may change the atmosphere of your home or workplace; this is the principal of sowing and reaping. Nevertheless, this type of human affection that we learn arises out of our soul and not our spirit. If we keep building on this premise of the soul we will miss God's plan, because we are building upon our soul life, which must ultimately be denied. We really have to see that we are corrupt to the core.

Therefore, the individuals practicing such an endeavor cannot produce love from within themselves. They may attain to a certain behavior that love produces, as we read in 1 Corinthians 13, but the behavior does not produce a source of love. *True godly love cannot be produced by work at all.* True godly love only comes from God through the person of His Holy Spirit, and we can only receive this love by admitting that there is no love in us to begin with! This is the very opposite of trying to attain love through the work of self-effort. If I work at "learning to love" and attain certain virtuous habits connected to it (which goes for any other practice) and see nothing more, I am in danger of a form of godliness entering my life. This will blind me from coming and receiving God's never ending source of love, because His genuine love can only be received through humility, prayer, and repentance. We must wait and receive God's Spirit to come into us, for He is love as the Father and Son are love. From that point we don't need to work at love, we will *become love*, for God's Spirit will *envelop* us in it, and shed it abroad in our heart as Paul said. Indeed, this is the goal.

Again, when we are immersed in the Holy Spirit, the virtue of love, for instance, doesn't need to be attained to, because it will "be" us and flow through us. It's a ridiculous notion to think that we can patch up our old corrupt nature and have love come out of it! Jesus was talking about the corrupt nature when He said, "You don't try to patch up an old garment with a new piece of cloth because they don't agree!" (See Mark 2:21.) In other words we must have our corrupt nature replaced with a new one: God's *own nature agreeable with Himself* living within us. Clearly this is an act of God outside of our *own power* to do it. Man must *stop striving* to create a godly life for himself out of the old, and allow God to give him a new life within. But who is willing to count the cost of bemoaning his own corrupt self till God comes through with His answer?

Therefore, this lifestyle can and has deceived many from coming into fullness, not only the ones practicing this, but many onlookers. The life looks incredibly pious and devoted; it may even create the suggestions in other people's minds, "I wish I could be that strong to achieve such godly virtues." The fact of the matter is that these are "dead as a doornail" works. *Dead works are produced by one's own strength.* This in itself suggests we are separating people into categories of who has a *stronger willpower,* which takes from the worldly mentality "only the strong survive"; only the strong can live godly lives. This was not God's plan; this isn't God's plan now and will never be God's plan. The Lord wants to put you on as His "coat of many colors." He wants to possess you so fully that every cell in your body is the Lord, and that you become the very fruit of God. This is true godliness and true virtue!

Chapter 11

HOW TO RECEIVE

HUNGER AND THIRST

FAITH HAS A completion in manifestation. One may argue that we need to "live out" what we seek by faith as if we have received. Don't be beguiled into less. Don't you dare stop pressing your claims at the court of heaven until you receive the full manifestation of your inheritance in Christ through the Holy Spirit!

When a child seeks bread in the Scripture, he isn't given a stone, which is dead; he receives the tangible bread that satisfies the body (Luke 11:11). This scripture is about satisfaction, being satisfied with the tangible substance of that which is asked for. Believing that you received by faith before the manifestation that Christ refers to in Mark 11:24 does not imply that once we have asked we go on pretending that it has happened without expecting a supernatural manifestation; to do this would be absurd! What Christ is saying is to be fully convinced in your mind without any doubt whatsoever that the manifestation will be revealed. In the meantime, you are to be as the widow towards the unjust judge (Luke 18:1–8), continually coming before God and pleading for your promise, pleading for your inheritance. Ask, ask, and continue to ask, as the man who came to his friend at night seeking bread and wouldn't leave till his friend "manifested" the bread into his hands. Continue to believe and proclaim you have received, yes, but *continue to press.*

It is so disheartening when I read a book and the author writes that God gave him or her the heart and mind to see what they needed. They prayed once and believed, but there was no manifestation in the end, only a claim to a light superficial experience. I always feel they have been robbed and their experience has little impact for others. Be honest, do you want to see and feel even more than we could ask or think manifested? Are not the people you want to admire those who see the mark and don't give up till the manifestation of God takes hold of their life in reality? Are they not the ones that kindle a fire in your own heart and cause you to say, "If they can do it, so can I"? You might argue that you are opening yourself up to manifestations from the devil. My question to you is, whose side are you on? Are you for us or for our adversary?

When we seek the full manifestation of the life of Christ, which God provided in the Holy Spirit, that we may be restored back to our original dominion and relationship with the Triune God, are we not praying for God's promise? What makes you think you would be led out of the protection of Jesus Christ and His blood, to "receive from the devil?" Ridiculous! Of all the human beings that ever walked the face of the earth, Jesus Christ was the most open to the manifestations of God, and the devil had nothing in Him. The greatest threat to the devil is a person who will take God at His promise and not take "no" for an answer till the thing becomes a manifested reality. These are the people who will destroy Satan's kingdom.

May I continue to press my point? Take a look at the faith chapter in the letter to the Hebrews (chapter 11). Those people who moved on in their faith always received the manifestation according to the faith exercised.

> But without faith it is impossible to please [God]: for he that cometh to God must believe that He is, and that He is a *rewarder* of them that diligently seek Him.
>
> —HEBREWS 11:6, EMPHASIS ADDED

What is God's reward if He is a rewarder? Is it not the manifestation of the thing sought for? Of course it is. Could this be why the church does not experience the life prescribed in the Bible, because she no longer presses diligently into the manifestation of God's promises till the breakthrough is made?

Christian life is to be marked by one supernatural manifestation of faith after another. Don't sell your faith to the idea that praying *once* means it is a done deal; if you do, you will "hang on" by faith. This causes you to be deluded, because over a period of time you lose the desire to see the full manifestation of God's answer become a reality. After waiting, maybe even years, you come to the dreadful conclusion that God doesn't want to give you His promise, that it wasn't for you after all.

Dear friends, do we hunger and thirst for faith? No. We hunger and thirst for the manifestation by faith. If you lose your *desire to receive* the manifestation, you lose your hunger and thirst for it. Do not think for a second that you are noble or pious because you can stand on God's promise without hunger and thirst. You may need to become "undignified." Bury your face in the dirt at the feet of Christ, and let your tears fall to the earth. Allow your desire to be so strong it bleeds forth to the heart of Jesus day and night till God breaks through in your life. Do not stop till you have "wrestled" with God and receive.

The "faithists" must realize that just as faith without works is dead, (James 2:26) so faith without manifestation is dead also! Kathryn Kuhlman says, as they tarried in the Upper Room, they received nothing by faith.[1] By faith they went into the Upper Room. By faith they accepted that which Jesus had promised. But their tarrying was mighty real, and when they came out of that Upper Room, not one of them had accepted that experience by faith. *Something really happened*!

If your faith is marked only by believing and not receiving, something is wrong, and you must discover what it is. God's promise for the fullness of life in Christ through the Holy Spirit is now in the present. Your destiny by receiving this fullness is to become a supernatural manifestation to the world. Believe it! If the *manifestation of God's promise* is not the goal to be hung onto, we are nothing more then hopeful dreamers. When the disciples went into the Upper Room, they went in by faith, yes, but came out in manifestation! If it is not so, Christianity merely remains good ideas.

Jesus said those who hunger and thirst for righteousness will be followed by the manifestation of being filled. Those who seek, ask, and knock (not once, but for as long as it takes), the manifestation will follow. If you hunger and thirst do not wane. In your prevailing with

God, do not say, "I have received, I have received," stopping short of the manifestation. Do not think God is displeased with you because you want to see, feel, and experience. God is not *two-faced*. He does not say, "Because you want a manifestation for your faith, I will withhold it from you." No! God wants you to hunger and thirst for the manifestation of His promise *so much* that your lively faith will receive.

Again, do not think that in your continual seeking, asking, and pressing you lack faith, because you simply don't believe enough. No. The very fact that you come before God with an unrelenting faith to receive allows Him to put the spirit of prayer upon you, that you may prevail on through to take hold, as a women travailing in birth with pangs to be delivered. Daniel prayed through for twenty-one days till he received his answer.

You may question, what is God's purpose in the waiting and prevailing? In it there is a time of searching and examining oneself in the light of the Holy Spirit, and on the other side God is drawing you into Himself, and drawing your desire for what you seek out. The extent of this drawing by God is done in accordance with the "greatness" of the gift of God for which we seek.

A couple illustrations may help you see this more clearly. Picture in your mind a balance; on the right side, the promise of the Holy Spirit weighs down the plate. You possess a bag named "faith," and in it are weights, which you can place on the left side of the balance. The weights have names like "time," "consecration," "fasting," "repentance," "obedience," "prevailing prayer," etc. As each of those are acted upon in your life, it is placed on the left side, which in turn begins to bring the right side up, until it is outweighed by the left side, hence the blessing is poured forth. One may say, "Are you not buying or earning the blessing rather than believing for it?"

> Ho, everyone that *thirsteth*, come ye to the waters, and he that hath no money; come ye, *buy*, and eat; yea, come, *buy* wine and milk *without money*.
>
> —ISAIAH 55:1, EMPHASIS ADDED

Simply put, we are using God's "economy," not based on *monetary value*, but on *hunger and thirst*!

The second illustration is of a son coming up to his sixteenth birthday; if the son asks for a car, what then? Well, a car is certainly worth more than a cake and requires responsibility. The situation may be that the parents don't require the boy to pay back the thousands of dollars it costs to buy it, but he may be given a set of tasks to acquire that vehicle as his own. Now if the son said, "No, I will ask once and not fulfill your conditions, but wait till you give it to me," what would you think if you were the parents? The boy doesn't really want the car! It is just a *dream*. He's not *willing* to put any *effort* into it. The same is true for God. Jesus Christ purchased with His blood "Life" for us by the Holy Spirit. He doesn't require us to pay for this gift with *our* blood, but our hunger and thirst, willingness, and effort for it must be at a level that satisfies the heart of God to receive.

∼

YOUR CONSCIENCE

And herein do I [Paul] exercise myself, to have always a conscience void to offence toward God, and toward men.
—ACTS 24:16, EMPHASIS ADDED

The conscience is something that isn't talked about, but is of great importance between establishing your relationship to God and receiving what you ask for from Him. Our conscience is the instrument that the Holy Spirit uses to convict us of sin or wrong conduct, past or present, and needs to be heeded. Jesus's first commandment that He preached was, "Repent: for the kingdom of God is at hand" (Matt. 4:17), therefore, one must repent. Let it be understood that this is no general repentance, "I'm a sinner, please forgive me God." No. It is our past that has been an offense to our conscience, involving God or God and man. Before we "know" Christ our conscience is *dead*, but through a true conversion it becomes *alive to God*. Take note also, conversion has nothing to do with being in the church. Remember, Peter walked with Jesus through His ministry, and the Lord still said to him after "the devil would sift him like wheat, "when you are converted." (See Luke 22:31–32.) Therefore, people can still believe in Christ and not have a conscience alive to God.

Begin by softening your heart and allowing the Holy Spirit to probe your conscience, and there will be incidents that will come to your mind from your past that God wants you to deal with. It is usually not difficult to determine what these things are, for they will come in the form of conviction. You will *feel wrong* about it; it will *continually return to your mind*, or you may even have *reoccurring dreams* about it. In most cases this has already been happening to people, but with *no teaching* there has come no relief. The fact of the matter is that God wants to purge your conscience so there is nothing stopping the relationship between you and Himself, and that your prayers are not hindered.

A good rule of thumb to follow is this: if something comes to your mind, then confess it before God and ask for His forgiveness through Christ. If the thing drifts away from your mind, losing its strength, and you forget about it, God has accepted your repentance. If it doesn't drift away then you need to take the appropriate action to make it right before your fellow man as well.

How does this happen? The Holy Spirit will require confession and sometimes restitution depending on what the situation was. This may seem like a difficult undertaking, especially if you are working through a multitude of things. But God wants what is best for you now and in the future, and there can be no hindrances to your receiving His fullness.

> Therefore if thou bring thy gift to the altar, and there rememberest that thy brother hath ought against thee; leave there thy gift before the altar, and go thy way; first be reconciled to thy brother, and then come and offer thy gift.
>
> —MATTHEW 5:23–24

Jesus commanded that if *you* remember go "*first* be reconciled to thy brother." Moreover, Zaccheus stood and said unto the Lord:

If I have taken any thing from any man by false accusation,
I restore him fourfold.

—LUKE 19:8

What was Jesus' response?

This day is salvation come to this house.

—LUKE 19:9

In the first scripture there is the requirement of confession (which leads to reconciliation) and in the second, restitution is made. In my own life I have made both confession and restitution. Over a period of over two or three years, I cleansed my conscience, which is a most *liberating* feeling; because of this it has been *strengthened*, so I immediately know if the slightest thing is *offensive*. In this, my conscience has become a true guide to me, and it is kept clean moment by moment.

One incident involved an individual who continually stayed on my mind, and I would dream quite frequently about this person *rejecting* me in some way or another. This went on for years, until I wrote a letter confessing my conversion to Christ, and the wrong that I committed toward them, asking in the end for their forgiveness. This person was not a believer, and I never heard back, which is not the point, because God required me to clear up the offense by writing the letter. To prove this, approximately two weeks after I sent the letter, I had a dream involving this person, in which I dreamt that I was accepted! I was given peace and no reoccurring or pressing thoughts have come to me about it ever since.

In John G. Lake's writings, there was a woman who shared this testimony:

"When I knelt down, I said, 'Jesus, what is the reason I am not baptized?' And Jesus would show me this thing and that thing that I must make right. Then eventually there was a final day when she asked, 'Why am I not baptized?' And Jesus told her that when she had written five letters to different ones who had wronged her and whom she held a grudge against, He would baptize her. So she sat down and wrote those letters, carried them out and mailed them, and came back and sat down. As she did so, the Holy Spirit came upon her and she was not able to move and sat there for six hours while the Lord talked to her."[2]

Do you see, the people had not even received the letters before she received from the Lord! It is God who requires us to cleanse our conscience, and as soon as we take the first step He is there to meet us.

Use these wrongs as a door to proclaim what Christ is in your life; that it is because of Him you are motivated to make things right. You may not get another opportunity, and if you put Him first He will go before you. I encourage you to let God have His way; it is vitally important to Him and yourself that your conscience be purged clean. For there is no wrong that seems too big, worth *holding onto*, compared to what God wants to *give you*, I can assure you.

Again, we read from Gerald Derstine's book *Following the Fire* a similar testimony:

"In the process of my pursuit of sanctification, I felt compelled to make restitution for anything in my life I had not taken care of before. The lengths I went to were extreme, but my mind wouldn't rest until it was done. I searched every nook and cranny of my past and uncovered other little skeletons. A towel I'd taken as a souvenir from a hotel on our senior high school trip to Washington, DC. A $25 dollar deposit on a car I'd kept when the potential buyer reneged. Different people I'd offended with my tongue or attitude. They all got calls or letters. It wasn't easy, but I didn't want any obstacles on my path to sanctification. My efforts were finally rewarded."[3]

I believe this is a place where the devil has been able to lie to many people, telling them that all these things are "under the blood." Remember, justification changes how God sees us, but the Scriptures make it clear that we are still held responsible for our actions. Then, Satan makes people think that these reoccurring offenses that keep resurfacing in their minds is the devil himself trying to keep them in a place of guilt! Yet no matter what, they find no lasting peace, fighting and cursing these thoughts and the devil and ending up defeated. This is the devil's trick to disguise the conviction of the Holy Spirit. It is the Holy Spirit who is trying to guide you into true liberty, but for this to happen we have to stop running from these things and face them head on.

Once we have made these issues in our lives right and receive peace from God, if the embarrassment of these things returns to plague us we can know that Satan is behind it. Please understand, I don't mean that every passing thought is God convicting you about something, or that you need to go and dig up things that are not coming to the surface by themselves. You must test them. If the thoughts remain and press and consume you, rest assured this is God, and you must deal with whatever these are. There will be bigger things and smaller things that need dealing with but don't get discouraged; one by one it will come to an end.

If when you have come to the end of cleansing your conscience and you feel that something has offended it but are not quite sure, wait. If the thought seems to disappear then this is not conviction; but if it returns to your mind often enough and weighs on your heart, deal with it; it is better to know that it is dealt with and finished than to let it be a breach between you and God.

This is one of the biggest traps set for the body of Christ to hold the church back from purifying herself. Don't let the devil hold you back from moving forward toward your inheritance in the Spirit of the Living God!

∽

CONSECRATED TO GOD

We must be consecrated to God in two ways: God-ward and people-ward. God must come first in all that we do. We must spend time in prayer and seek Him diligently, reading and studying His word, living by it, up to the light given to us! He must be prominent in our lives. Jesus said:

> Seek ye first the kingdom of God [each day], and His righteousness.
>
> —MATTHEW 6:33, EMPHASIS ADDED

Consider Solomon:

> So was he [Solomon] *seven years* in building it [God's temple].
>
> —1 KINGS 6:38, EMPHASIS ADDED

Then it says:

> But Solomon was building his own house *thirteen years.*
>
> —1 KINGS 7:1, EMPHASIS ADDED

At a quick observation you would say that the temple was finished six years before Solomon's own house, for a total of thirteen years. But look at what it says next:

> And it came to pass at the *end of twenty years,* when Solomon had built *the two houses*, the house of the LORD, and the king's house.
>
> —1 KINGS 9:10, EMPHASIS ADDED

Solomon was not building up his interests and forging ahead with his own plan alongside of God's. No, he built the Lord's house first, then his own house. We must do the same. In building God's house first we learn to "deny ourselves, take up our cross and follow him" (Matt. 16:24-26). For in losing our life to put God first, we gain His. I'm not suggesting that you quit your job or sell all that you have, or stop moving forward with things in the natural world to put God's interests first. There are specific timings for these things, and they must be properly discerned. Paul says:

Let your moderation [avoiding extremes] be known unto
all men.

—Philippians 4:5, emphasis added

What we are dealing with here are the motives of our heart in
putting God first. The Lord can only move in our lives when we come
to grips with the fact that there is nothing in this world that can satisfy
us like God's reality. When we do see that the world is *dead* to us,
our responsibilities in it are done with no emotional attachment to
them; and when this happens, your desire to apprehend Christ's life is
where your emotions will ultimately lie. Therefore, God can give you
the desire of your heart because the world has been severed from it.
The greatest commandment is:

Love the Lord your God with all your heart, with all your
soul, with all your mind, and with all your strength.

—Mark 12:30, nkjv

We must go through each day so mindful of God and His inheritance
for us in Christ that it becomes such a present reality in our heart that
our spirit will become strong in faith, vision, and hunger to secure it.

As the hart panteth after the water brooks, so panteth my
soul after thee, O God.

—Psalms 42:1

∼

Your Gifting

God also wants us to first use what He has already given us through
Christ, and, as good stewards, be diligent with it.

Having then gifts differing according to the grace that is
given to us, whether prophecy, let us prophesy according to
the *proportion of faith*.

—Romans 12:6, emphasis added

In other words, use your gift to the level you have been given right now. A greater impartation is not likely to occur until you wisely trade what you have. Remember the parable of the talents:

> And unto one he gave five talents, to another two, and to another one; to every man *according to his several ability*; and straightway took his journey. Then he that had received the five talents went and *traded with the same*, and made them other five talents. And likewise he that had received two, he also gained other two. But he that had received one went and *digged in the earth*, and hid his *lord's money*.
> —MATTHEW 25:15–18, EMPHASIS ADDED

We must trade the "Lord's money" (our particular gift) in His "economy" (His body) to receive two or five "other talents" (increased gifting). It is usually the one who has received little; the "one talent" (non-spectacular gift) that sees himself or herself as "little." Yet as I have been stressing, God's promised Life and Power through Christ in the Holy Spirit is the same for all; but it may take stewardship with the "one talent" in the beginning to get there. Take note also that this is the "Lord's money" given to you. Therefore, it is not yours to keep and hold on to; you are obligated to use it, and if you do so willingly you receive a reward. As Paul states:

> For if I do this thing [preach the gospel] willingly, I have a reward: but if against my will, a dispensation of the gospel is committed unto me.
> —1 CORINTHIANS 9:17, EMPHASIS ADDED

When you think you are ready for the next thing in God, you need not beg and plead and hold your breath before Him to try and strain out the answer for the next step. But rather ask yourself, have I neglected trading the "Lord's money" (gift) within me and left it dormant either through ignorance or avoidance (which most often springs from fear)? Or, have I outgrown what I'm doing with my "talent" presently; have I grown up to the next step?

God will never take us out of children's clothing till we have outgrown it! He will not allow the cart to be put before the horse or allow a detour in the road to move ahead. If you are pregnant with the vision that God has for your life, there's the tendency to birth this vision by *C-section* and bring it forth our own way. We must first take every measure to utilize the gifts God has given us at present, giving them forth and pouring them out with all our heart. By doing this we would not only grow in maturity, quicker than we could imagine, but walk into our next set of clothing spiritually, as naturally as a child grows into new clothing physically; so much so that taking thought for the next step in God becomes *non-existent*, because one walks from one revelation in Christ to another.

Most of the time we look *beyond* to a farther step than we can reach right now, and out of fear, *hold back presently* so we do not accomplish it rather than giving all that we have to the particular thing at hand, and finding out that the equipping for what lies ahead comes without conscious thought of it. This is being led by the Spirit in the truest sense, and is the point at which God begins to trust *you*. Christ grew up in the Spirit as naturally as His physical body did. Just as the scripture says, "He grew in favor with God and man." His life was a continual dawning, not a constant wandering. Jesus gave all that He had, to receive all that He could from the Father.

There are talents and gifts that were placed within us from the dawn of time in the mind of God that are as natural to us as the air we breathe. They are who we are, woven into us for our destiny. Most of the time, growing up in God simply means doing the most natural thing for us "*spiritually*," letting out what God has put in. Thank God and use what you have right now with all your heart, and your life will be catapulted beyond any of your predecessors.

You may question, how do I do this? You can do this once you know your gift or giftings, through revelation or prophecy or that you know, that you know, that you know. Receive the words that Paul wrote to Timothy:

> *Neglect not the gift* that is in thee, which was given thee by prophecy, with the laying on of the hands of the presbytery. Meditate upon these things; *give thyself wholly to them*; that *thy profiting may appear to all*.
>
> —1 TIMOTHY 4:14–15, EMPHASIS ADDED

In other words, *promote* your gift; please understand I'm not talking about a prideful boasting about what you have been given. If the gift is truly from the Lord there will be no need for flashing lights and a neon sign that says "me, me, me." One thing that will always go before God's gifts is a humble spirit that does everything it can to be unnoticed. Instead, what I am talking about is looking for openings and opportunities where it may be used. If there is someone or something trying to put a cork on your gift, uncork yourself; the world is larger than four walls! Look for a place or places where it is accepted and let it grow into something larger. It may take some time to find those places and for God to open up doors, but He will if He sees your willingness. Jesus compared the spirit life to the world around Him in His teachings. Your *gift* in the Spirit is like a *skill* you possess in the world. When you look for a job do you forget or bury your existing skill and look for a job that you have no skill in? No! You use the skill you possess and look for the opportunities that will reap the best benefit and be the most effective. Timothy was probably a timid person, especially because of his youth (1 Tim. 4:12), but Paul exhorted him to *take his place*. In Paul's own case, he says:

> Woe is unto me, if I preach not the gospel!
>
> —1 CORINTHIANS 9:16

If we all viewed our giftings that way there would be *room made* for us. I want to put emphasis on this because you may have prayer and the Word in balance in your life, but this is where confession of Christ fits in, and where you fit in edifying the body of Christ.

> A man's gift maketh room for him, and bringeth him before great men.
>
> —PROVERBS 18:16

The unearthing of your gift may be as simple as discovering what you desire in your heart *the most*. God is a God of order. Your gift will be what you want to do and use. It may not bring you the fewest difficulties, but it will bring you the most satisfaction. Your gift is what *inspires* you, and what you can envision yourself doing. Being diligent with these things mentioned will increase your hunger for His fullness in the Holy Spirit and will give you the right to storm the courts of heaven to be quickly answered. Let's move on to the next chapter and see how these things fit together for us according to Old Testament.

Chapter 12

THE FEASTS

ROM WHAT HAS been said already, let's look at the spring feasts in the Old Testament to see how these conditions tie together (Lev.23:4–22). The first feast on the Jewish calendar is Passover, on the fourteenth day of the first month. We know that Jesus is our Passover Lamb and we find our covering for our sins in His shed blood as explained in the chapter on justification. Faith in Christ through personal acceptance marks a beginning point in our new life with Him. This in a sense would be our "personal Passover."

Let's move onto the feast of unleavened bread. One day immediately following the Passover feast in Scripture, the feast of unleavened bread begins.

> Seven days shall ye eat unleavened bread; even the first day
> ye shall put away leaven out of your houses.
> — EXODUS 12:15

And in verse 19 we read:

> Seven days shall there be no leaven found in your houses.

The custom of the Israelites (which evolved from the Lord's commands) was to take a candle representing God's light, a feather representing the Holy Spirit, and a spoon, and do an entire spring cleaning of their house to sweep up all the little crumbs of leaven found. They would use the light of the candle to find the crumbs, then sweep them up with the feather onto the spoon and carry them out of the house. The leaven is what represents inward-known sin, sin that is visible by our conscience's "eye" that has been sitting there in the corners of our houses! It must get out! Look at what Paul says:

> *Purge out therefore the old leaven*, that ye may be a new lump, as ye are unleavened. For even Christ our Passover is sacrificed for us: Therefore let us keep the feast, *not with* old leaven, *neither with* the leaven of malice and wickedness; but with the unleavened bread of sincerity and truth.
>
> —1 CORINTHIANS 5:7–8, EMPHASIS ADDED

Note that Paul makes an *important distinction* here between "old leaven" and the "other leaven" of malice and wickedness. The old leaven represents something already lying around, something from our past, which must be purged, made a clean sweep of, while we are purging the outward leaven at the same time! As I said before, this is what liberates your conscience, removing all obstacles between you and God.

God also commands the Israelites to eat unleavened bread to complete the seven-day feast. Why is this important? This shows us that this is not an easy task, but it is important in God's eyes. The Jewish people call this bread the "bread of affliction," and when you eat this bread for seven days, you know why! It is a *hard thing* to do; there is *no delight* in it. Jesus was afflicted for us and bore our shame (Heb. 12:11), so when we are converted to Him we must bear our own shame for the things we have done wrong and get the leaven out. For further proof of this, we can ask *why* did God make this feast an ordinance in the first place?

> For in this selfsame day *have I brought your armies out of the land of Egypt.*
>
> —EXODUS 12:17, EMPHASIS ADDED

A few things to note here: first the Israelites were still inhabitants of Egypt when God said, "This self same day have I brought [you] out." The Lord was speaking *future tense*; it was already "done" in God's eyes regardless of their *present citizenship*. Therefore, the doing of it is a done deal; in other words it must be done. Second, when they left Egypt they were thrust out speedily and no time was allowed for leavening bread (Exod. 12:39); hence this was not a time for thinking things over and lingering about, but a time for "doing" in haste to get out of Egypt. Third, Egypt is symbolic of sin and the environment and influences that surround sin, which required urgency to get away from. From these three points the Lord is telling us that we must cleanse all leaven out, past and present because in His mind it is *already done*! We must do this in haste without tarrying so we can be set free from the stain of Egypt, our old way of life of sin and influence, which includes cutting off old company that still promotes a sinful life.

In this Jesus is also our pattern, He was taken into Egypt against His own free will (Matt. 2:13–14), because he had no will of His own, being yet a young child. Then we read:

> Out of Egypt have I called My Son.
>
> —MATTHEW 2:15

It is stated in a way that sounds like Jesus could lead His way out by His own will, yet we read in verse 21 that He was still a young child! Of course He was a little older, but still did not possess a will of His own, because He was led out *by Joseph*. What is the Lord saying? Well, let's see the parallel in our own lives regarding Christ and what God commanded the Israelites. Jesus was led into Egypt to prove that the stain of sin would be placed upon Him, but God called Him out to establish a sinless life. God called His Son out in future tense just as the Israelites in Egypt! Jesus was *obligated to fulfill this*, which He did. Then we read in Revelation 11:8 that Jesus was crucified in Sodom and *Egypt*, which once again represents sin. We were made sinners not by choice, but by the genetic fall of mankind against our free will! Do you realize that Jesus was so identified with us that it wasn't in His power not to become sin for us?

> For He hath *made Him to be sin* for us, who knew no sin.
>
> —2 CORINTHIANS 5:21, EMPHASIS ADDED

He was first *led* into Egypt, then He was *made* sin. Both times not having a free will of His own, but needed God to deliver Him still.

> Who in the days of His flesh, when He had offered up
> prayers and supplications with strong crying and tears
> unto Him that was able to save Him from death, and was
> heard in that He feared
>
> —HEBREWS 5:7

We were infants born into sin, Jesus was an infant led into sin, the Israelites were born into slavery. We trust God for deliverance from sin through Jesus. Jesus trusted God for deliverance from the sin put upon Him; the Israelites' prayers came up to God and He heard them. We must understand this point, that Jesus was called out of Egypt (sin) as a "done deal" just as the children of Israel and so are we. The old leaven must be purged out as quickly as possible, just as the feast of unleavened bread immediately follows Passover. God puts this as your task immediately after conversion; your personal Passover. The seven days which are allotted show us that God allows a little time to clean our houses and move on to the bigger picture. The next feast is the feast of firstfruits.

> Ye shall bring a sheaf of *firstfruits* of your harvest unto the
> priest: and he shall *wave the sheaf of the first fruits* before
> the LORD, to be accepted for you.
>
> —LEVITICUS 23:10–11, EMPHASIS ADDED

Rabbis still teach that if you want God to make bread you have to bring the barley sheaf, or don't even ask Him. Therefore God was setting a principle for us: bring your "first" fruit and wave it; take your initial "talents," the first little bit of gifting the Lord has given you and wave it; make it visible, so He can begin to do something with it, i.e., "make bread" out of it. Then the Word says:

> Offer...an he lamb without blemish of the *first year*.
>
> —LEVITICUS 23:12, EMPHASIS ADDED

This is the *second* "first" mentioned; this represents giving the best of you and what you possess. Also take note that it is a single animal required, because you don't have a lot at the beginning. Let's continue:

> And ye shall eat neither bread, nor parched corn, nor green ears, *until* the selfsame day that ye have brought an offering unto your God.
> — LEVITICUS 23:14, EMPHASIS ADDED

This is another "first" principle. You must put God first; you must offer to Him first, seek Him first. This is your consecration.

The Israelites were then given seven weeks or fifty days to bring in the harvest. This period of time characterizes our developing in character and what God has given us. It's a time of being "sifted like wheat," and is also a time of growth and maturity in our gifts and consecration. It's a time of giving out what we are taking in, a time of feeding others by what has been given us, as we see here:

> Thou shalt not make clean riddance of the corners of thy field when thou reapest, neither shalt thou gather any gleaning of thy harvest: thou shalt leave them unto the poor, and to the stranger.
> —LEVITICUS 23:22

Matthew 11:5 prophetically shows that Jesus is the "harvest" of God. He took in all of God, produced the fruit and did not gather up the corners of His field but preached the gospel to the poor. This brings us to the next point: the harvest resembles abundance and by taking our "firsts" we are to be getting ready for that "abundance." We have been getting rid of the old, preparing and making "room" in our "storehouses" for the full reaping of the harvest! Now you have been working long and hard to get prepared, and somewhere in there from the beginning to the end of the harvest you've gotten mighty hungry to see your work completed, to celebrate and move on to other tasks.

The last feast of spring is called by three different names: the feast of weeks which is the completion of those seven weeks; also known as feast of harvest and Pentecost. God calls this the "firstfruits of thy labors" (Exod.23:16), which is a fitting description, *making the completion of our "firsts."* Feast of harvest represents the totality of our labors that have ended in the abundant rest of God's provision. Pentecost, which is the Jewish festival Shavuot, marks the Law being given to Moses on Mount Sinai, which has been skillfully woven into this feast. The Lord foreknew that the giving of the Law would fall on the same timetable as the feast of weeks, or by its other name, the feast of harvest, in the future. God is telling us that one day our "labors" will be completed by His Law of Life written into us, Himself descending into us. Beautiful! And for centuries He was painting a historical picture to prepare the people to receive it. Don't you see the greater significance and depth God is revealing to us about the Gift of His Life in the Holy Spirit? Furthermore, Pentecost was one of three feasts in the calendar year that all the males of Israel were required to attend. This is a message for the church today: Jew and Gentile, small and great, male and female; *all members of Christ's body must not miss God's abundant provision!*

Now the offering to God at the feast of harvest is noteworthy:

> Ye shall bring out of your habitations *two wave loaves* of two tenth deals; they shall be of fine flour; they shall be [baked] *with leaven*; they are the firstfruits unto the Lord.
> —LEVITICUS 23:17, EMPHASIS ADDED

In verse 13 they brought God the *raw ingredients*, the first fruit out of the field. The sheaves, which represent the beginning of our labor and effort, involve what we *must do* and what we must *deal with*. Now, we see in verse 17 that they brought two loaves to be waved. Why? This is the "finished product" of our work and God's work; when we do our part God "couples it" with His! Also, the bread was baked with leaven; doesn't leaven represent sin? It is used in two ways: yes, for sin, but also for *satisfaction and fullness*.

The *kingdom of heaven is like unto leaven,* which a woman took, and hid in three measures of meal, till the whole was leavened.

—MATTHEW 13:33, EMPHASIS ADDED

The people asked Jesus:

Whence hath this man this wisdom?

—MATTHEW 13:54

Wisdom was hidden inside till the kingdom of God was leavened within Him! I believe that we must give God the raw goods of our lives, and by passing through what is expected of us, purifying ourselves and putting God first; He alone is capable of leavening the bread within us, which is meant to be broken to feed a multitude. Just think: "five loaves" within *you* could feed five thousand, besides woman and children!

∾

Now let's summarize the spring feasts:

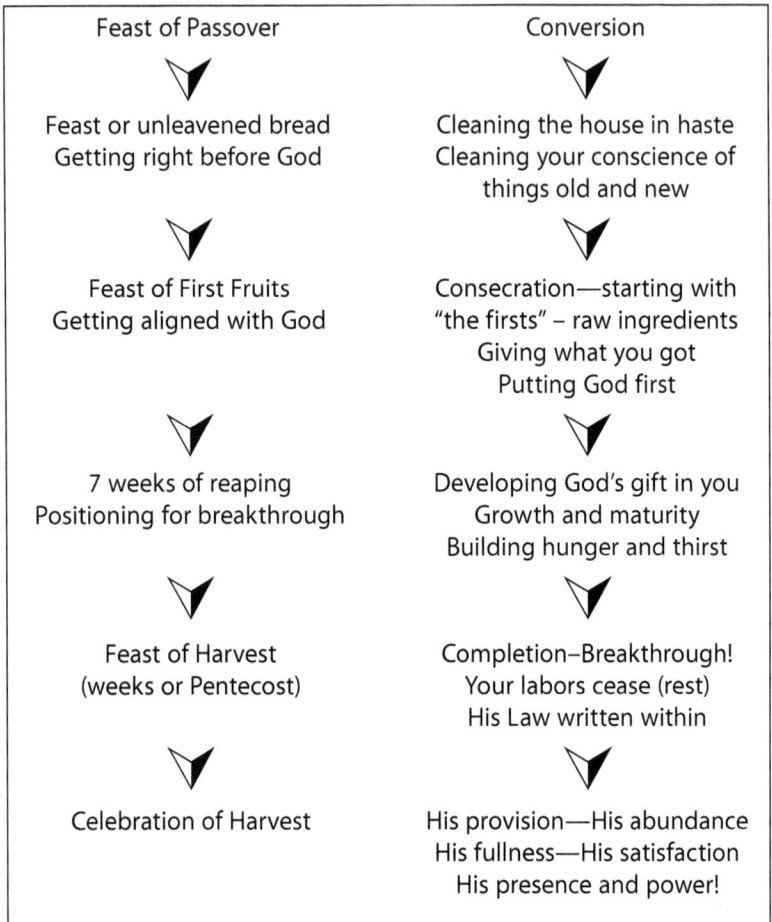

Feast of Passover	Conversion
▼	▼
Feast or unleavened bread Getting right before God	Cleaning the house in haste Cleaning your conscience of things old and new
▼	▼
Feast of First Fruits Getting aligned with God	Consecration—starting with "the firsts" – raw ingredients Giving what you got Putting God first
▼	▼
7 weeks of reaping Positioning for breakthrough	Developing God's gift in you Growth and maturity Building hunger and thirst
▼	▼
Feast of Harvest (weeks or Pentecost)	Completion–Breakthrough! Your labors cease (rest) His Law written within
▼	▼
Celebration of Harvest	His provision—His abundance His fullness—His satisfaction His presence and power!

Through this picture given to us from the feasts of Passover to harvest we can clearly see that there was a definite process established by God to secure His promise of abundant life in the Holy Spirit. We should not herd people to get them to receive; otherwise we can be duped into receiving something far less than the full reality of God's promise. We must walk through each appropriate action for God to give us His end result.

This process is very personalized, and God works with each person individually to take the proper steps for breakthrough. It is as person-alized as the outpouring experience itself. We have to realize that as much as God wants people to receive His promise to walk in His full-ness, He is equally interested in cleansing us and causing us to become responsible stewards, that His presence and power may embody us.

This is an incredibly heavy responsibility and to be taken with utmost seriousness. God will not give this to babes and to those playing superficial games, yet this seems to be the way people think God will do it, taking no thought for what stage the individual's per-sonal walk is at or the condition of his or her heart. If we really exam-ined the way we think God gives out His most precious Gift, I think it would be easy to see that there is little truth in the widely accepted methods of today.

As adults we would not deal with our own children in the way we think God should do this for us, and unfortunately many people go through this life missing the entire reward. Let's stop just "doing church" and give God our best, staying on Him and what He has promised so we can receive His best.

I will reiterate once again, there is a path that God has shown us to walk on, but there are *specific conditions* that must be fulfilled indi-vidually for God to give us His promise. If we do not fulfill those con-ditions in all our lifetime, God will not deviate from the requirements He has for us, and we will not cross over our Jordan into Canaan. For some this may be the valley of decision; is it time to make a cap-tain and return to the mind-sets ingrained within from the land of familiar, or march forward and take hold of the land of promise?

Chapter 13

THE DAY OF ATONEMENT

L ET'S LOOK AT the symbolism of the Day of Atonement to further assist us in understanding our preparation between firstfruits and Pentecost.

On one hand we have laid down our life for God, yet on the other, there still remains sins, self-will, bad habits, character issues, disobedience, rebellion, and so forth.

> And Aaron shall cast lots upon the two goats; one lot for the LORD, and the other lot for the scapegoat. And Aaron shall bring the goat upon which the LORD's lot fell, and offer him for a sin offering. But the goat, on which the lot fell to be the scapegoat, shall be presented alive before the LORD, to make an atonement with him, and to let him go for a scapegoat into the wilderness.
>
> —LEVITICUS 16:8–10

We see that there were two goats presented before the Lord; one goat was slain for a sin offering, the other goat had the sins of the people transferred onto it and was let go into the wilderness. The slain goat is your identification with Christ's death, and your commitment to offer your sins to God and become wholly His. The scapegoat is you in your actual state with the self-life that still remains; but this goat is not slain but released into the wilderness. Why? The same reason the Israelites were turned back from entering the Promised Land into the wilderness.

This generation was not ready mentally or in character, therefore their carcasses needed to die in the wilderness; this is symbolic of our sin and self, those things which we can overcome by putting them to death. When all the old Israelite generation died (which was a long, drawn-out forty-year process), it opened the way during that time for the "Joshua generation" to be *perfected*. Therefore, there were two companies of peoples: the first generation was to be "slain" and the second generation was to be perfected for the Lord's work. The old had died, taking Egypt to the grave with it, and the new had arisen "who knew not Egypt"; hungry, thirsty, and restless for the Promised Land. They were prepared mentally but also perfected in faith, trusting in God and obedient to the statutes of the Lord. You will always have to taste death to get you hungry for Life, but not unlike the Israelites in the wilderness, death (i.e., lifelessness) has become a familiar friend, and we pitch our tents of compliancy here, setting up camp for generations to come. This is a strange thing.

The perfection of this new generation is seen by the immediate judgment of the Lord upon Achan in Joshua 7:16–26. There was nothing muddling the way to clear victory so when there was a single offense, it was clearly seen. This is exactly what happens when we have cleared the way to victory in our *own conscience personally*. This is the purpose for the scapegoat; we are given space to repent and die on the one hand, and are rising up in perfection on the other.

Jesus was not only our Passover Lamb whom we follow to our own cross, but also the pattern of the scapegoat being sent into the wilderness by the Holy Spirit. Why? To be proved that His own will, His own "self" had died in exchange for God's purpose, God's Promised Land. We also must understand that in Jesus's days of submission and obedience *prior* to the wilderness He learned to remain under the authority of His earthly parents and under the rabbis of His day. He learned to choose the good and reject the evil, and also learned the scrolls, the Law, and the Prophets, to defeat the devil and live by their rules. Hence Jesus showed Himself approved and became strong in the Word and in character, as we must do.

In this season between firstfruits and Pentecost we learn the pain of self-denial and submission, continuing to make choices for God and His direction. Does your job afford you no time? Make a transition in careers and be content with "food and raiment," our daily necessities (1 Tim. 6:7–11). Is your life too busy? Maybe it is a portion of sleep you have to deny yourself (Ps. 132:3–5), or a social function you must cut off. This is *preparation time*, redeem it! We can't receive the Holy Spirit's abundant life and power without these things being established in our lives. We still have a free will after the Holy Spirit takes full possession of us; our lives have to be conditioned and trained to automatically minister to God. We must be in His reins, surrendering to His guiding bit in our mouths; otherwise we could end up being spiritually full but physically lazy, basking in His restful bliss. No, God will not allow this to happen; you must be in line with His order.

Behind the scenes before Jesus's reception of the Holy Spirit and public ministry, He was being trained in a personal ministry towards the Father. Do you think that Jesus only ate when he was hungry or prayed all night or recited the written word because the Holy Spirit was upon Him? No. These disciplines were already a part of His life, which is why the Holy Spirit, could come and why His ministry abounded.

> And Jesus increased in wisdom and stature and *in favour with God* and man.
> —LUKE 2:52, EMPHASIS ADDED

Do you think He got there by some special power? No. He got there the same way we must.

> Though He were a Son, yet *learned He obedience by the things which He suffered*; and being made perfect, He became the author of eternal salvation unto all them that obey Him.
> —HEBREWS 5:8–9, EMPHASIS ADDED

Do you think this suffering that taught Jesus obedience was the cross? No; because at the Cross there was no time for "learning." Christ's suffering was in His self-denial and self-abasement, and the Cross was the consummation of *that* obedience which he had learned. By this He became "The Christ," the Author of eternal salvation.

Jesus passed through every progressive step in His own flesh to fulfill the Father's will that is laid out for our own lives. He walked the path first and gained the victory to prove that He was making the New Life in God's Spirit absolutely attainable!

Therefore, we need to accept the Lord's chastening of ourselves (Heb 12:6), although it may be grievous (Heb. 12:11), that we may willingly walk in God's ways and put His interests first. God's promised Holy Spirit is His pearl of great price. Now it's up to you to receive your harvest from heaven, the only place of genuine experience. Don't settle for less!

Chapter 14

SUMMARY

Justification -First washing -First Fruits	The acceptance of Christ's atoning blood to cover our sin, enabling us to stand before God, blameless and cry out to Him.
Period of Grace -7 days -7 weeks	A measure of the Holy Spirit is given to work with us through repentance, breaking off of the old life and purging our conscience

Most of the body of Christ has stopped right here. Unfortunately, because of insufficient teaching about what is expected and lack of willingness to hear and obey, this stage is very rarely walked through thoroughly. As good in itself as Justification might be, it only leaves an expectation of Heaven. The church of Laodicea prided herself in having "life," but in actuality there was only spiritual *unreality*, having religious duties and forms to fill up the hinder part of "lukewarmness" and complacency. This is where church socialism becomes the focus, stirring up a fury of activity with things to do, but lacking real power.

Period of Grace (cont.)	Using and exercising what God has gifted us with becoming a good steward and trustworthy in the things God has given us; growing and developing in them.

Some in the body of Christ have moved to this point, but have allowed their gift to become the *total sum* of their destiny, not recognizing the *true purpose* of God. The devil lies in wait to draw them out of relationship and discipline of the Lord, convincing them that by the operation of their gift they are in right standing with Him, causing them to think of themselves more highly than they ought.

Period of Grace (cont.)	To realize the total depravity of our inherited sinful nature. To stir up a great hunger and thirst to be "like" God, set free from the blemish of sin, crying out day and night. To submit under the Lord's hand and total self-abasement.
Sanctification	
-Jesus's baptism of fire	God's holy fire from the altar of heaven burning and purging everything that isn't of Him.
-Sin offering of Ourselves	Cleansing us from the mark of sin and all that defiles us. Cleansing the house for the Holy Spirits indwelling Person and Presence.
Glorification	
-Second washing -Harvest of fruit that remains -Pronounced clean -Baptism in the Holy Spirit	Triune God making their abode in cleansed man through the person of the Holy Spirit. Keeping, preserving, and sealing them in God's presence, holiness, and state of sinless perfection identical to Jesus. God's filling and replacing man's sin nature with His own divine nature and characteristics. Restoring and making whole; the completion of Man.

Those in the body of Christ who are granted passage over to this existence know their God and know the true purpose of His salvation and Sonship. It is these who will do exploits; they are granted to sit with God and are given the keys of the kingdom, sharing His power, authority, and dominion in the earth and in heaven. They have passed from religion into life and reality. Many are called but few are chosen! *It's up to you!*

ENDING PRAYER AND EXHORTATION

I BELIEVE THAT THE church of Christ has been waiting to have questions raised and confronted about the present weaknesses in her. I believe there is a longing in her for a generation to rise up and raise the bar on the reality and truth of the Christian life. I believe the Lord God Almighty has been wading through the darkness of His body waiting for the trumpet call to enlightenment.

I believe the Lord is weary with self-serving sacrifices and the compromises to live in stagnant waters. I believe the Lord is longing for a generation to stir those still waters and create a tidal wave of hunger and thirst. I believe with all my heart that if we get the Lord's purpose right as the early church did, everything would fall into place and no one would feel neglected; the sons of glory would be manifested, drawing the curtain closed on the end of the age.

I pray that the enemy is forbidden to steal this word out of your heart and harden it:

> My people are destroyed for lack of knowledge: because thou hast *rejected* knowledge, I will also reject thee.
> —HOSEA 4:6, EMPHASIS ADDED

The Lord is saying the knowledge was there, but the sin was in the rejecting of it. May it not be so in this day and in this hour.

I pray that as you close this book the burning of God would begin, if it hasn't begun already, and continue to burn in your heart as a witness, not letting you rest until you have encountered God in this divine manifestation of the Holy Spirit within you. Let Him have His way and search you. It was disobedience that brought the blemish of sin upon man. It is only obedience through the love of God, willingness, and desire to see God's will be done that can get us back. Let us not be disobedient to the heavenly vision and neglect the totality and fullness of Christ's salvation.

Smith Wigglesworth says, "Pentecost is the last thing that God has touch[ed] the earth with. The baptism is the last thing; if you do not get this [right], you are living in a weak and impoverished condition that is no good to yourself or anybody else."[1] Everything that has taken place in history up to the present comes down to one common denominator in the heart of God: God inhabiting man; man possessing the fullness of God! This is the Key!

2 Acts: Coming Soon to a City Near You

In the days of the end there was an assembly raised up by the Lord Himself. God called them His sons of power, for they did not hearken unto the voice of man, nor were they persuaded by the will of man; but hearkened to the voice of the Lord. They knew who they were, for the Lord put within them to know. It was these who were free; pulsating with the life of God's Spirit. They were beholden to nothing but their Bridegroom Jesus Christ. God did test them thoroughly, and found their hearts to be perfect before Him and unwavering; therefore God restored their lives as it was before man's fall, and granted them unlimited power to glorify His Name and His dwelling place in the earth. They caused the nations to tremble at what they saw, but their focus was clear: Christ's return.

We don't need another revival; we need a revolution!

NOTES

CHAPTER 4
THE ISSUE OF SIN

1. Gerald Derstine and Joanne Derstine, *Following the Fire* (Plainfield, NJ: Logos International, 1980), 55.

2. Edward Read, *Studies In Sanctification* (Salvation Army, 1975) 3–4.

CHAPTER 5
THE ISSUE OF SIN CONTINUED: THE PLAGUE OF LEPROSY

1. *Merriam-Webster Dictionary 50th Anniversary Edition* (Springfield, MA: Merriam-Webster, Inc., 1994).

CHAPTER 6
DNA AND THE GENETIC FALL OF MAN

1. *Funk & Wagnalls Standard Desk Dictionary* (New York: Harper & Row, 1984).

2. http://en.wikipedia.org/wiki/File:DNA-structure-and-bases.png (accessed July 1, 2011).

3. *NOVA*, "Cracking the Code of Life."

4. Ibid.

CHAPTER 7
THE FULLNESS OF GOD IN MAN

1. *Merriam-Webster Dictionary 50th Anniversary Edition* (Springfield, MA: Merriam-Webster, Inc., 1994).

2. *Maria Woodworth-Etter: A Complete Collection of Her Life Teachings*, comp. Roberts Liardon (Tulsa, OK: Albury, 2000), 43.

3. Smith Wigglesworth, *Smith Wigglesworth On the Holy Spirit* (New Kensington, PA: Whitaker House, 1998), 21.

4. Smith Wigglesworth, *Smith Wigglesworth On the Holy Spirit* (New Kensington, PA: Whitaker House, 1998), 16.

5. *John G. Lake, The Complete Collection of His Life Teachings*, comp. Roberts Liardon (Tulsa, OK: Albury, 1999), 368.

6. Kathryn Kuhlman, *The Greatest Power in the World* (North Brunswick, NJ: Bridge-Logos, 1997), 52.

7. *John G. Lake, The Complete Collection of His Life Teachings*, comp. Roberts Liardon (Tulsa, OK: Albury, 1999), 71.

8. *Funk & Wagnalls Standard Desk Dictionary* (New York: Harper & Row, 1984).

CHAPTER 8
SCRIPTURAL EVIDENCE: WHAT REALLY CHANGED?

1. Bonnie C. Harvey, *Charles Finney: The Great Revivalist*, Heroes of the Faith (Uhrichsville, OH: Barbour, 1999), 46.

CHAPTER 10
STOPPING SHORT

1. Smith Wigglesworth, *Smith Wigglesworth On the Holy Spirit* (New Kensington, PA: Whitaker House, 1998), 89.

2. Dwight L. Moody, *Spiritual Power* (Chicago: Moody Press, 1997), 85.

CHAPTER 11
HOW TO RECEIVE

1. Kuhlman, *The Greatest Power in the World* , 61.

2. John G. Lake, The Complete Collection of His Life Teachings, comp. Roberts Liardon (Tulsa, OK: Albury Publishing, 1999), 420.

3. Gerald Derstine and Joanne Derstine, *Following the Fire* (Plainfield, NJ: Logos International, 1980), 53–56.

ENDING PRAYER AND EXHORTATION

1. Smith Wigglesworth, *Smith Wigglesworth On the Holy Spirit* (New Kensington, PA: Whitaker House, 1998), 115.

ABOUT THE AUTHOR

THROUGH KARL LOESCHER's life experiences God was preparing him to seek a deeper revelation of the truth and depth of wisdom on this subject that isn't being taught in the church today. For this reason this has caused Karl to draw closer to God on this matter and not farther away. Over a period of fourteen years Karl has allowed this revelation from the Lord to grow and slowly take root, through the study of God's Word, reading other Christian authors, prayerful meditation, and inspired conversation among Christian believers.

After a season of prayer the Lord spoke to Karl and asked if he would write for Him now. In obedience Karl began writing this manuscript at the end of 2008. Through severe financial hardship and trials of pressure, *Thirsting for Life and Reality* was completed in the summer of 2009. Another two years passed as Karl prayerfully meditated on and polished what had been written while waiting for God's arm of provision to complete this work in 2011.

Karl's desire is to see the preparation of the Lord's bride and the equipping of His people. You can read about Karl's miraculous conversion also to be released by Creation House Publishing. His testimony will inspire readers and give them a clear path of repentance and deliverance resulting in a meaningful lasting walk with the Lord.

CONTACT THE AUTHOR

I welcome your comments

and hearing from you

Please e-mail

shareyourcomments@gmail.com

∿

To contact the author

e-mail Karl Loescher at

backtonewlife@gmail.com

∿

As the trumpet call is beginning to sound,

There is a voice crying in the wilderness in these days,

"Make straight the way of the Lord's second coming!"

Your destiny awaits!